THE WAY HOME

ENDING HOMELESSNESS
IN AMERICA

THE WAY HOME

ENDING HOMELESSNESS IN AMERICA

PHOTOGRAPHS BY JODI COBB, BENEDICT J. FERNANDEZ, DONNA FERRATO, BETSY FRAMPTON, TIPPER GORE, ANNIE LEIBOVITZ, MARY ELLEN MARK, ELI REED, JOSEPH RODRIGUEZ, STEPHEN SHAMES, CALLIE SHELL, DIANA WALKER, CLARENCE WILLIAMS

CURATED BY PHILIP BROOKMAN AND JANE SLATE SIENA

FOREWORD BY TIPPER GORE

ESSAY BY NAN ROMAN, PRESIDENT, NATIONAL ALLIANCE TO END HOMELESSNESS

HARRY N. ABRAMS, INC., PUBLISHERS, NEW YORK, IN ASSOCIATION WITH THE CORCORAN GALLERY OF ART, WASHINGTON, D.C.

The Way Home: Ending Homelessness in America has been organized by the Corcoran Gallery of Art, Washington, D.C., in collaboration with the National Alliance to End Homelessness. The exhibition is funded in part by a generous grant from RiteAid, Inc., with additional support from Eastman Kodak, Inc., Dodge Color, Inc., the AFL-CIO Housing Investment Trust, the Communications Workers of America, and Dr. Louis W. Sullivan.

On the binding: detail of a photograph by Benedict J. Fernandez, page 47
On the title page: detail of a photograph by Jodi Cobb, page 29

Edited by Eve Sinaiko
Designed by Ana Rogers

Library of Congress Cataloging-in-Publication Data

The way home : ending homelessness in America / photographs by Jodi Cobb . . . [et al.] ; curated by Philip Brookman and Jane Slate Siena ; foreword by Tipper Gore ; essay by Nan Roman.
    p.   cm.
  ISBN 0-8109-4553-3 (hc)
  1. Homeless persons—United States Pictorial works. 2. Homeless persons—United States. I. Cobb, Jodi. II. Brookman, Philip.
III. Siena, Jane Slate.   IV. Corcoran Gallery of Art.
HV4505.W27 2000
305.569—dc21   99-38450

Photographs on pages 2–3, 22–31, and jacket back © Jodi Cobb; photographs on pages 44–53 and binding © Benedict J. Fernandez; photographs on pages 86–95 © Donna Ferrato; photographs on pages 76–85 © Betsy Frampton; photographs on pages 6, 66–75, and jacket front, above © Tipper Gore; photographs on pages 126–131 © Annie Leibovitz; photographs on pages 32–43 © Mary Ellen Mark; photographs on pages 10–21 © Eli Reed/Magnum Photos, Inc.; photographs on pages 96–105 © Joseph Rodriguez/Black Star; photographs on pages 116–125 © 1999 Stephen Shames/Matrix; photographs on pages 106–115 © Callie Shell; photographs on pages 132–141, and jacket front, below © Diana Walker; photographs on pages 54–65 © Clarence Williams/Los Angeles Times.

Poem on page 17 copyright © 1999 James Mann; poem on page 24 copyright © 1999 Elizabeth Anne Newton; poem on page 46 copyright © 1999 Larry Kyle; poem on page 65 copyright © 1999 Neal Avery, Jr.; poem on page 68 copyright © 1999 Larry Mitchell; poem on page 84 copyright © 1999 Caverly Stringer; poem on page 89 copyright © 1999 Gregory C. Hill; poem on page 105 copyright © 1999 Randolph Shaird.

Printed and bound in the U.S.A. by The Stinehour Press, Lunenburg, Vermont

ABRAMS Harry N. Abrams, Inc.
100 Fifth Avenue
New York, N.Y. 10011
www.abramsbooks.com

Once homeless, this gentleman is now part of a community in Miami (the photographer, Tipper Gore, is visible at left).

It's been said that a journey of a thousand miles must begin with a single step. But for those who are homeless, that single step must feel like an insurmountable distance to travel. This book is intended to help illustrate the journey. We've learned so much about solutions in the struggle to move people out of homelessness. Providing a roof over their heads is important, but individuals face multiple needs. Often, the agony of the abject poverty represented by homelessness is a symptom of additional, equally deep problems, such as mental illness, chronic illness, drug or alcohol addiction, the experience of catastrophic loss, or other traumas.

Many Americans are living in a time of great prosperity. We have the strongest economy in a generation and have achieved a balanced federal budget for the first time in thirty years, with the largest monetary surplus in our history. Yet here is a stark fact: On any given night 750,000 people face life on the streets; more shocking still, 150,000 of them are children. As we begin the new millennium, I believe that each of us—at every level of government and in every community—has an individual obligation to contribute to shaping our nation's future. And part of that process is deciding the fundamental question of national values: Will we use these good times to widen the circle of dignity and prosperity—to bring light into the dark corners of our nation that are too often neglected? Or will we let compassion fatigue divert us from the simple fact that every one of us can make a difference?

In every city and town across America, there are individual heroes whose service as volunteers helps this country strengthen its sense of community, bridge our differences, and build the foundations of a stronger, more cohesive society. These heroes come in many shapes and sizes. They are the members of a local parish who spend a few hours every week dispensing warm clothing to homeless people. They are the children who collect canned goods from home to take to school to help feed hungry classmates. They are the people working on the front lines of humanity every day to provide for those less fortunate.

I understand the impulse to turn away from someone who is homeless, to avert our eyes to the tragedy that can sometimes seem overpowering. When the problem of homelessness began to arise in the 1970s it was easy for me to look away. My husband, Al, was serving in Congress, and I was busy raising four young children. The problem seemed so distant to me. What could I, one person, do to help?

Things changed. One day I was driving with the kids when we saw a homeless woman standing on the curb, talking to herself and gesturing. The kids noticed her and wanted to know why she was there. When I explained to them that she was probably homeless, they were horrified and immediately asked to take her home with us. Seeing her through their eyes helped me to realize how long I had averted mine when I encountered homeless people. That evening, the family sat down together to figure out what we could do. We started by volunteering for a local Washington organization that provides food for the homeless. In 1994 I also began to give time to another Washington organization that provides health care for the homeless.

This nonprofit program is a mobile unit staffed by people who know the city's homeless population as well as you or I know our next-door neighbors. Every day they traverse the city in a van, dispensing medical attention and social services. They also encourage the people they encounter to enter a continuum of care—shelters, clinics, residences, outreach centers, and day programs. Pat was my companion on my trips in the van. She is one of the quiet heroes, who has worked out of a residence for homeless men since the 1980s to help our capital's homeless population. She makes the rounds regularly, checking up on the homeless people she knows, making sure they are healthy, and always, always trying to convince them to come in for help. When I cannot join her, she sends me notes and updates on those she calls "Tipper's treasured friends," to help me keep up with how people are doing.

I believe in one-on-one advocacy. The hardest thing about convincing fragile and anxious people to seek help is earning their trust. The mobile-unit volunteers are able to do this. It can take weeks, even months or sometimes years, of meeting and talking to get to know someone individually before he or she will trust you enough to let you help.

Jack lived in a wooded area in Rock Creek Park. He was extremely shy. On several visits he resisted our efforts to help him, but after a few tries, he would sit in the van to talk. At first, when we were able to persuade him to come back with us to the shelter, he would again leave immediately. Gradually, though, he began to stay long enough to have a meal or a shower. One day I got a call from Pat, because it had been a long time since she had seen him. When I heard that Jack was missing, I began to look out for him. A couple of days later I was jogging in Rock Creek Park and spotted him, asleep on a median strip. I convinced him to go to the shelter for a shower and treatment with a medicated shampoo that is used for head lice, and he did, but halfway through the application he suddenly decided to leave. The next thing I knew he was running down the street, his hair bristling stiffly with the shampoo, while we dashed after him. He gave us the slip, and we were all very worried for fear of what the strong chemicals in the shampoo would do to his scalp. That night, Pat found Jack back on his hillside. He was disoriented and clearly a danger to himself at that point, so they took him into supervised care. For a while, he was in a hospital for the mentally ill, where I visited him several times. He started taking medication and has since moved to a permanent group home, where he has now been living for the past two years. Recently he told me that he is back in touch with a brother and sister who live in Japan.

Jack's improved circumstances are a real success story. Captain Kersh is another. He is a Vietnam War veteran who lived for many years in Farragut Square Park, in downtown Washington. He was quite difficult to talk to, resistant and isolated. I got through to him by telling him that my husband had been in Vietnam too, in the Army Twentieth Engineering Brigade, and eventually I convinced him to move into the shelter temporarily. I learned that he was owed ten thousand dollars in accrued veterans' benefits, now being held in a trust for him. After some eight months he was doing so well that the staff decided to move him into transitional housing. To progress from a shelter to more stable supervised housing is a key goal of outreach, but it can be difficult for some. The prospect apparently frightened him so much that he ran away the night before he was supposed to move. Pat alerted me, and I went looking for him. I found him in the park, and as I had expected, he once again needed to feel the security of a connection to other veterans. I handed him a note I had asked Al to write to him that morning. It said:

> Dear Captain Kersh,
> You should go back to Christ House and to Anchor Mental Health. This is a temporary housing solution for you. I am very proud of the progress you're making.
>
> > Your fellow Vietnam veteran,
> > Al Gore

He agreed to return to the program and in the car on the way he told Pat, "The Vice President of the United States, second in command of the whole country, is telling me I have to go. So I have to do it." Making a personal connection is such an important part of reaching out.

One day in Lafayette Park, which is right across the street from the White House, I came across a woman who was obviously suffering. I asked her how I could help and she told me that she needed to "get her reality back." She said her name was Mary Tudor, so I let her know that we shared the same first name (Mary Elizabeth is my given name) and that we were meant to be friends. I asked her if she would come with me to a facility that provides transitional housing for people in crisis with mental illness. She explained that she was waiting for her husband, and that if she left he wouldn't know where to find her. Her husband, she said, was President Clinton. I had an idea. I told her that I knew how to get a message to President Clinton. We walked across the street to the guard post at the West Executive Avenue entrance to the White House. The officer on duty recognized me, but I signaled him not to show that he knew me. I introduced Mary and told him that she was a friend of mine who was coming with me to a mental-health program. I asked if he would please inform President Clinton that she was safe. This satisfied her and she came with me and got the treatment she needed. Today, she is restored to health, working full-time for the federal government, and living in shared housing.

There are so many reasons and causes for homelessness. I remember Jeffrey (not his real name), who lived under one of Washington's many bridges. He was dying of AIDS. He had spent some time in a hospital, but he knew he was dying and wanted to be in a place that felt like home. For him, that was under the bridge with his friends, who were also homeless. I spent several days sitting with him and just listening as he talked of his life, his hopes and dreams. He passed away, but is not forgotten.

Carl was a young man who had left home at an early age. He had begun abusing drugs but tried off and on to get clean. When I met him, he talked about his children. He had two kids the same age, and I remember exclaiming, "Oh, you have twins!" and he laughed at me and explained that they were children of different mothers. One day he decided that he really needed to see his mother, who lived down South. I offered to buy him a bus ticket, although Pat worried that he might sell it for drug money. But she called me later that day to say that she had dropped him off at the bus station, so I went to see him off. We shared a cup of coffee and talked about his family and his ambitions for the future. Then he got on the bus and headed home.

I am a great believer in helping those in need one-on-one. You're much more effective that way, and the satisfaction you get is much greater when you personally give of yourself. If you write a check, you will do great good, but if you never connect directly with the people you want to help, you will never feel as fulfilled as you will if you take the time to forge a real relationship.

So I try to keep these relationships strong. Pat sends me updates on my treasured friends and we get together from time to time to see how everyone is doing. I do get discouraged sometimes, since when people are ill and vulnerable for every step forward there are often many steps back. When that happens I remember the words of a child quoted in a book called *No Place to Be: Voices of Homeless Children,* by Judith Berck. Kareem, a young boy, said: "I really like when the lights go off in the movies because I'm no longer a 'homeless' kid. I'm just a person watching the movie like everyone else."

Let's never forget that simple principle—that we are all people, with human frailties, with beauty, with longing, and with need. Let's help each other find the way home.

CURATORS' STATEMENT

The Way Home: Ending Homelessness in America is a photographic exploration of one of the most important social problems now facing this country. There are many complex issues that lead to and define homelessness. Our perception of these topics and how they are presented allows us to understand them better. Our current knowledge of homelessness comes from photographs, movies, television, and print media, as well as from direct experience. Therefore, photographs can inform, educate, and interpret our embrace of these issues.

This exhibition connects us to the real world but interprets it in multiple ways. One of the roles of the artist in our society is to reflect on the realities of the times. *The Way Home* extends and builds on this tradition of socially focused art. After all, photography is a powerful tool that helps us make sense of what we see and experience. Photographs document our world—its troubles and beauty together—creating images that can be widely distributed in many forms. They blend both subjective and objective points of view to inform our feelings and understanding of what we see, making our collective memories visible. Traditionally, photographers have produced photo-essays or picture stories about relevant topics to help readers travel to pictorial worlds they cannot reach on their own. Often published in magazines or books, these essays provide moving and engaging insights into the lives of culturally and geographically diverse people.

The Way Home is a collaboration between the Corcoran Gallery of Art, the National Alliance to End Homelessness, and Harry N. Abrams, Inc. It follows the exhibition *Homeless in America,* a 1988 project at the Corcoran organized by Families for the Homeless and the National Mental Health Association, which drew attention to the human drama of homelessness. *The Way Home* builds on this history to convey a contemporary look at the issues that lead to homelessness in light of innovative solutions pioneered over the past decade. Its goal is to enlighten, to educate, to investigate both problems and solutions that lead to economic stability and permanent housing for everyone.

There have been many compelling images of men, women, and children who live in this country without a permanent home. Yet the faces of these people, presented as individuals, have become increasingly distant as their numbers have increased over time. For this project we engaged a group of outstanding photographers who each brought different perspectives, approaches, and styles to the subject of homelessness. Most of the work presented here is new, created between February and May 1999 in towns across the United States. To place the new images in context, some were selected from the archives of photographers who have long been interested in this issue. We encouraged photographers to break cultural and stylistic stereotypes so that homeless people might speak for themselves. *The Way Home* offers a simple, essential message: Homelessness is not a permanent part of American life. It can be solved.

It is impossible here to thank everyone who made this project possible. We must, however, acknowledge the significant contributions of a few. The many providers of services to homeless people gave us access to communities across the country. Many people who confront life without permanent shelter shared their stories. Each of the photographers contributed his or her time, images, and words. The staffs of the publisher, the Corcoran Gallery of Art, and the National Alliance to End Homelessness have woven the pieces together. An essay by Alliance president Nan Roman offers a clear-eyed look at the issues and programs. The poems in this book present creative voices of homeless men and women, most of whom are members of the Miriam's Kitchen Writers' Forum, Washington, D.C.

Philip Brookman
Jane Slate Siena
Curators

ELI REED

San Francisco has a long history of confronting social problems and caring for its people. But now its economic base has changed and even many middle-income families find housing too expensive. Time after time I have seen people in the city carrying telltale plastic bags, carryalls for meager possessions such as soap or toothpaste. When I approach to ask about their lodging they often respond, "Oh, I'm not homeless!" but usually admit within minutes that they are living in a car, or depending on the kindness of friends for shelter.

Advocates for homeless people are doing battle for the soul of their city. In a downtown restaurant south of Market Street every employee is or was homeless. In the Tenderloin district there are quiet art classes for homeless people that produce an impressive number of serious artists. Unfortunately, it has also become normal for pedestrians to pass by the city's homeless people daily, ignoring them as if they were familiar phantoms. And every day, the heart of San Francisco dies a little more.

Eli Reed photographed in San Francisco, California, in 1999.

Imhotep Narcisse, 26, homeless since the age of 14 and a gang-banger in the past, now writes songs and rap lyrics. He is sitting on a park bench near City Hall Plaza, a hangout for homeless people.

During the night limousine drivers talk near a homeless person's sidewalk dwelling.

Left: Carri "Babs Bunny" Grey, 22, on Haight Street in the Haight-Ashbury district.

Gavino Bantocino, a Philippine World War II veteran, in the room he shares with five other Philippine vets in the Tenderloin district. When these men came to the United States they hoped to receive benefits for the help they gave American troops during the war.

Market Street: In the early morning hours some homeless people sleep at the entrance to this mattress and bedding store.

A homeless man sits on a downtown Market Street perch.

Above: A worker at the Conard House 9th Street Cafe cleans up at the end of the day. All the employees are or were homeless.

MIRIAM'S KITCHEN
JAMES MANN

Numbers are given out
one by one,
On some days
number thirty-two,
On other days no number.

Finding a place to sit depends on the number.

Eggs, grits, and greens on one day,
Blueberry pancakes on Tuesday,
French toast on Thursday,
Coffee every day . . .

Why do they play musical chairs?

"Numbers one through ten!"
A line forms.
The numbers are not in order yet.
All the numbers are fed.
The food disappears and no more coffee.
The numbers are rearranged.

The doors are closed and no one can enter.
The numbers wait for the next day.

In the Tenderloin: Merrill Anderson, 23, is Native American, originally from a Navajo reservation in Arizona. He has been homeless off and on for six years. He found the statuette of a nun in Chinatown. He panhandles and sells found objects to get by.

A program called Mercy Charities Housing California found housing for the Carmona family.

Far left: Philippine World War II veterans live together in housing in San Francisco's Tenderloin district. One vet lives in a closet, together with his wife of over fifty years.

Near left: Aleksey Dygenny and his wife, Luvleov, both 73 and originally from Ukraine, have been married for fifty-one years and live in Folsom Street housing managed by the Mercy Charities Housing California program.

JODI COBB

Miami glows with light. It pulls impoverished immigrants from southern countries, tantalizing them with glittering images of riches and freedom. And it pulls the dispossessed from northern states with its warmth, color, and the sense that somehow life will be sweeter and kinder in the sun. For too many, it is not.

As I met Miami's homeless people, I found myself intrigued by the edges of their lives, the grace notes of survival: a touch, a toy, a picture on the wall. These details dignify a life—or degrade it.

Miami's outreach workers are not pictured here, but they made these photographs happen. They cruise the streets of the city, practicing their art of gentle persuasion, even putting money from their own pockets into the hands of homeless people, though they're not supposed to. But here's their secret: Many were homeless themselves once. They know well the people they help. They know their fears and denials. And they know these difficulties can be overcome. They are living proof, living hope.

They also know in their very souls that everything in life is temporary, that many of us are just a paycheck away from crisis, that fortunes change. So they take nothing and no one for granted. They love their job. They are true heroes.

Jodi Cobb photographed in Miami, Florida, in 1999.

The outreach team calls him Chinaman, the Asian man who wanders Little Havana. He never speaks, just smiles and nods. I asked him where he was from and he whispered, "Korea."

CROW'S DAWN
ELIZABETH ANNE NEWTON

Dawn's here, dawn's here
Tiny birds chirp in soprano
It's light, it's light
Crows in base tones
Cracked tone says
Wake up, the sun's coming
Over the housetop
Far off in the distance
A train whistles
Says goodbye to night
My restless half-slept
Night is over
I crawl out of the sleeping bag
Not too pleased with
The birds' chorus.

Left: Homeless people have taken over an abandoned apartment building in Miami's poorest and most dangerous neighborhood and made it their home.

Below: A woman sleeps in an abandoned building in Overtown.

Previous pages: Part of downtown Miami has an incongruous, tropical war-zone feel, with pastel-colored abandoned buildings and sleeping figures strewn about the streets.

Above: A late-night applicant arrives at the security gate of Miami's Homeless Assistance Center.

Right: This notorious alley in downtown Miami is abandoned by day, but by dusk fills with dozens of homeless men and women.

Opposite above, Miami Beach: Stephanie Palmer and John Healy hold tight.

Opposite below: A new arrival takes the hand of an older resident at Miami's Homeless Assistance Center.

Above: A new resident reaches for a toy at Miami's Homeless Assistance Center.

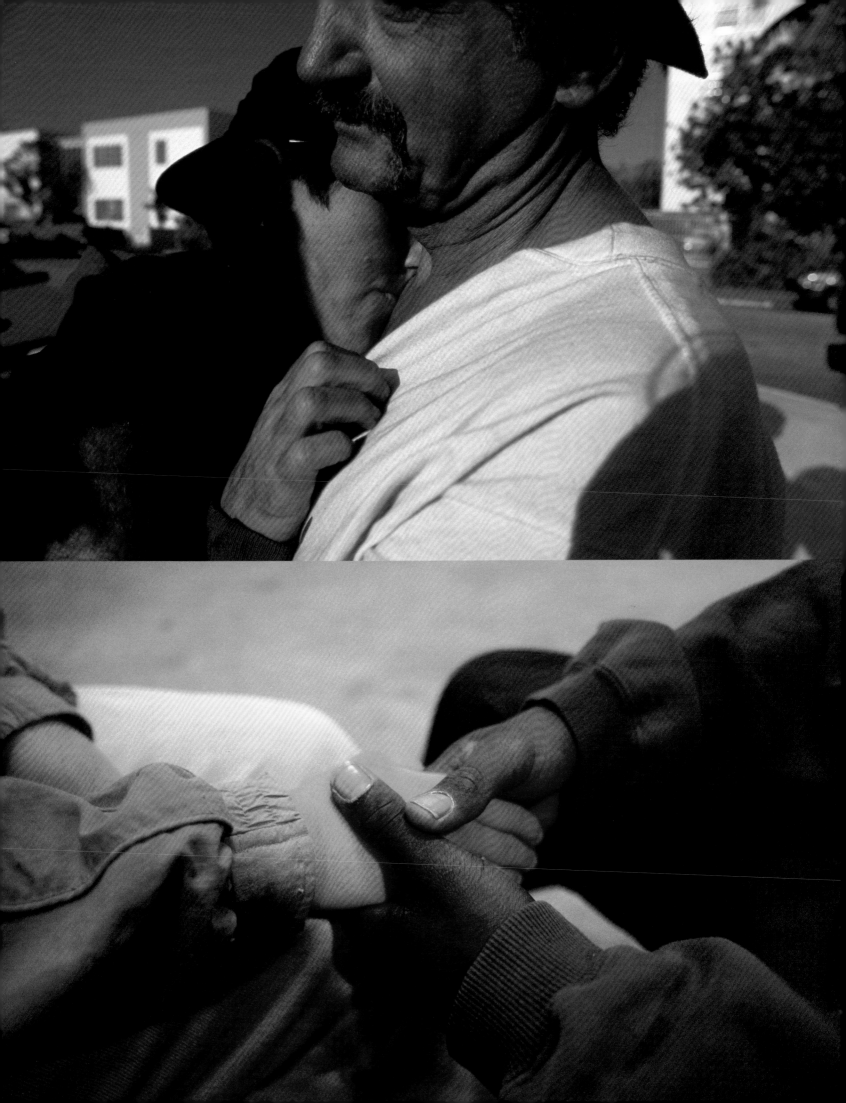

MARY ELLEN MARK

Being a social-documentary photographer for so many years has educated me. It has made me realize how unfair the world is. I wish that all people had equal opportunities. I realize how difficult it is to break the cycle of poverty. In several photo series I have focused on urban and rural poverty, drug abuse, runaway teens, and the shelter system. Recently, I have been looking at organizations that help provide solutions to some of these problems, including New York's Times Square residence and the HELP USA program (Housing Enterprise for the Less Privileged), a model program founded in 1986 that supplies housing and medical support for homeless people and uses existing government resources in a practical way.

Mary Ellen Mark photographed in New York, Kentucky, California, Florida, and Nevada, in 1987, 1993, 1994, and 1999.

The Damm family living in their car, Los Angeles, 1987.

Stacy Spivey and her baby brother, McKee, Kentucky, 1990.

Hector, Jessica, and Pablo Sanchez playing cops and robbers at a HELP USA site in the Bronx, New York, 1993.

Handing out clean needles in the South Bronx, 1987.

Andrea and Anthony Garrett at a HELP USA site in the Bronx, New York, 1993.

Kelly Flores on Halloween at a HELP USA site in the Bronx, 1993.

Tony Congema in his room at a HELP USA site, Suffolk County, New York, 1994.

Dannielle Watson with his dogs, Angel and Baby, at the Times Square residence,
New York City, 1999.

Haskell Rightor III, musician, Times Square residence, New York City, 1999.

Michael Kelly in a children's shelter, San Francisco, 1995.

Carrie Kuhn with one of her birds at a homeless encampment, Las Vegas, 1991.

BENEDICT J. FERNANDEZ

"Willie" lives in a condemned, burned-out Houston house he calls home. It's rent-free and he hangs out in the neighborhood with a number of others in the same situation. They begin their average day with a visit to a church where they can get a hearty breakfast. Then they look for used bottles and soda cans to turn in for deposit money, or stand between cars at traffic lights, asking for change. We see Willie in every major city in America.

In the afternoons he goes to an agency called Project SEARCH, where he gets his lunch, takes a shower, and can ask for medical care. Some evenings he goes to the Star of Hope mission, where he's entitled to a bed one night a week—if there's room—and a shower. This is a day in Willie's life. His reference points are different from what we may consider the norm, his attitudes more tolerant. He appears to have adapted to this lifestyle with ease, and shows no regret.

Perhaps Willie feels that his lifestyle gives him freedom from society's constraints. Should he give up this independence? His homelessness is a state of mind.

Benedict J. Fernandez photographed in Houston, Texas, and Washington, D.C., in 1999.

Houston: A man sleeps safely in the crevice beneath a highway overpass.

SPEAK SOFTLY SNOW

LARRY KYLE

The starlings have grown silent
That perch overhead
Just soft whispers
Before they rest in bed.

The snow is falling
Like angel dust
So soft and light.

Tonight I sleep with nature
My sheets are clean, smooth, and white.

Left: A man sleeps in a cardboard box in a parking lot in Houston.

Below: A homeless encampment in a Houston parking lot between two highways.

Right: A teenage mother and child at the Houston Salvation Army's shelter for families.

Below: The steel entry door to Project SEARCH, Houston.

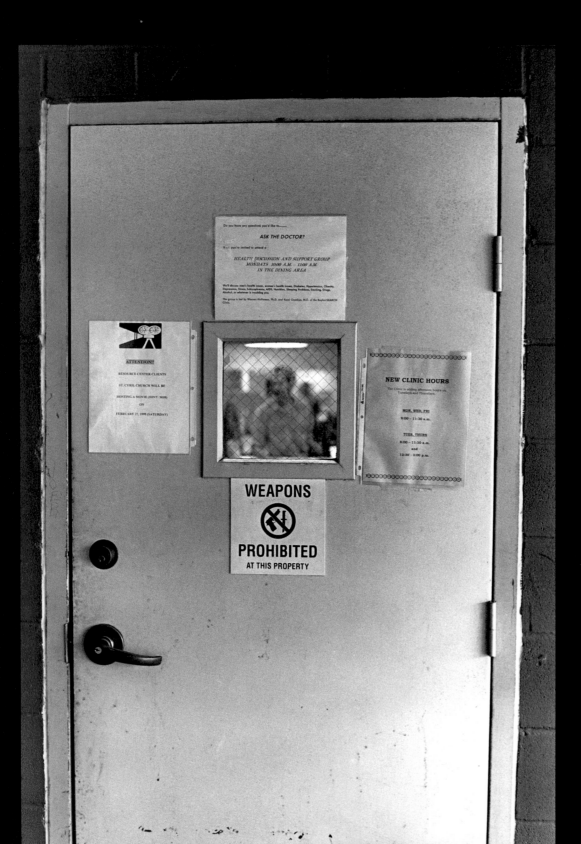

An early arrival at the Star of Hope shelter in Houston spends a little time playing solo chess.

A squatter stands in a burned-out, abandoned building in Houston.

Above: Hot coffee is breakfast near the Capitol, Washington, D.C.

Right: A homeless man spends the night atop a Washington, D.C., steam grate to keep warm.

CLARENCE WILLIAMS

Toward the end of 1998 I was assigned to do a photo-essay for *The Los Angeles Times* about medical care for homeless people. I met Gilbert Saldate, a street-outreach worker for a project called Homeless Health Care Los Angeles. Like most men and women who operate on the front lines of this battle, Saldate goes far above and beyond his job description. As I photographed him, I quickly learned a primary lesson of ending homelessness: that we must treat the whole person. The problems of people living on the street are complex.

Leonard Thompson, 44, a homeless amputee, and his friend Kelly Martin, 36, lived for quite some time under the Cesar Chavez Bridge, just east of downtown Los Angeles. Life under a city freeway exit is dirty, sad, and troublesome. Their lives continued in a destructive cycle, even as Saldate helped them. Heroin and crack cocaine remained a priority for them; prostitution and panhandling remained their usual employment. That next hit of crack or slam of heroin often set them back ten steps for every step forward that they took. Nevertheless, with Saldate's remarkable support, Leonard and Kelly are no longer living on the street.

Clarence Williams photographed in Los Angeles, California, in 1998 and 1999.

Leonard Thompson, homeless in Los Angeles.

Far left: As Leonard takes a sponge bath in his outdoor living room, one of his friends injects heroin.

Near left: A young woman briefly escapes from her family to visit homeless friends.

Kelly shoots up. Health care for homeless people is a tough issue. For hard-to-reach patients, social and psychological problems are so bound up with physical status that it is impossible to separate the strands.

Left: Kelly Martin looks at the contents of her purse.

Kelly, somewhat dejected after a day of being high. The Los Angeles skyline looms behind.

Gilbert Saldate talks with Leonard and Kelly under the freeway. His first goal is to interest them in finding help. A program for drug addiction, counseling, skills training—these things will come later.

Leonard playing craps in his open-air living room.

Kelly and Leonard.

Leonard cashing his first disability check in 1999.

Above: During a visit to the East Los Angeles Department of Social Services building, Saldate is momentarily overcome with emotion after finally getting Leonard disability benefits. He was eligible to receive this income during the six years he was homeless; through Saldate's efforts he began to do so.

NOMAD

NEAL AVERY, JR.

Needless things are in my way, I cast some of them away.
On good days they return, like a boomerang thrown the wrong way.
May the God spirit see fit to kill this thing that rises inside
And decides to try to depress me.
Digging down inside, I've found the strength to carry on without the things that return
*   like a boomerang thrown the wrong way.*

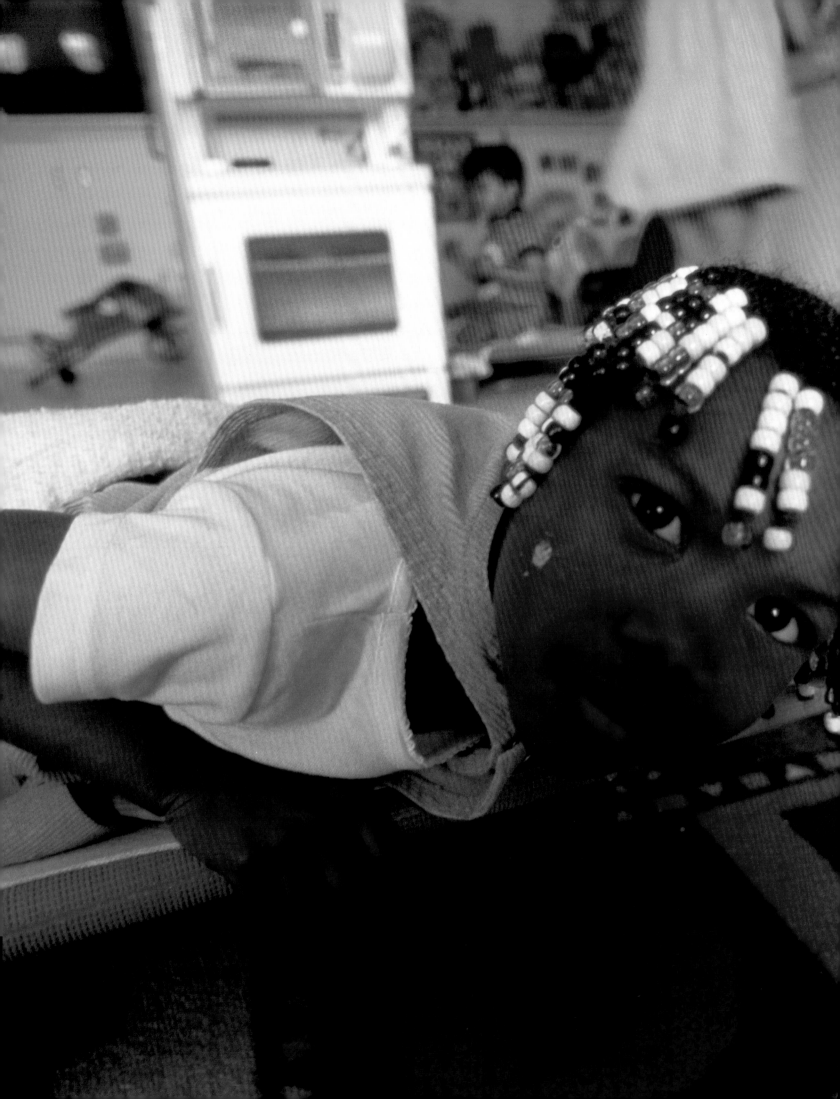

TIPPER GORE

I have met, through my work, many men and women who are homeless. The friendships we have shared have given me so much. These people have inspired me with profound respect for how individuals can manifest strength and dignity in the midst of adversity. Watching their struggles, I have been better able to understand the effect that isolation from family and community can have on any of us, from the most destitute to the most privileged. And through watching their successes I have been even better able to understand the power of the human spirit to triumph over setbacks, when it is supported by caring individuals and by the wider community.

I believe photography can be a powerful medium to illuminate the most complicated and controversial subjects. Photographs can touch the soul and motivate people to take action.

I am always deeply aware that each subject is a human being, a complex individual, not just an illustration of "the homeless problem." The people in these photographs want us really to see them; to give the lie to the notion that homeless people are an abstract social problem. Their faces, I hope, will help call each of us to action. We each have a role to play in creating a future in which America is truly home to everyone.

Tipper Gore photographed in Washington, D.C., Miami, Florida, and Tennessee, in 1974, 1995, and 1999.

A young resident at the Homeless Assistance Center, Miami, 1999.

RAIN
LARRY MITCHELL

To me like Stars

Above, Nashville, 1974: Evicted for not paying her bills, Hazel was put out on the street with her belongings. Here, she gathers her things and crouches beneath

Pages 70–71: The 1999 tornado season claimed thousands of houses and businesses, and many lives. In Clarksville, Tennessee, national historic landmarks and family homes were equally vulnerable. This Roman Street home, completely destroyed, typifies the widespread and indiscriminate devastation caused by natural disasters. It also reminds us that homelessness can happen to us all. After such events, Clarksville and other affected towns across America must rebuild entire communities—homes, churches, schools, parks, and workplaces.

Left, above and below: In 1995 a group of homeless people formed a family, creating an open-air home under the Whitehurst Freeway in Washington. D.C., not far from the John F. Kennedy Center for the Performing Arts, just at the edge of Georgetown. Their immaculate home and possessions were carefully organized and maintained, reflecting their sense of belonging and commitment to one another. They created their own social structure and environment as they did their best to manage their lives.

Right: The outreach workers at Douglas Gardens Community Mental Health Center in Miami Beach introduced me to Connie, who lives on the street, in 1999. She washes in public restrooms and takes meals in soup kitchens. We had a good visit while I took pictures of her and she talked about her life.

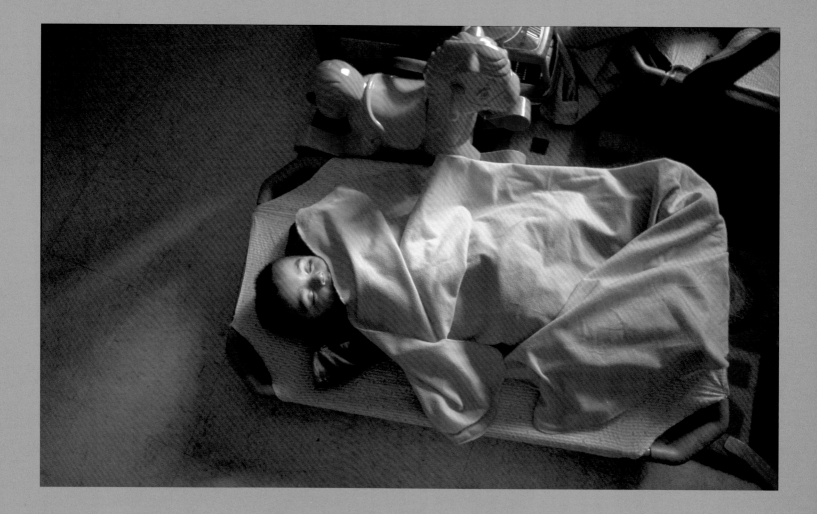

A quiet place, nap time, at the Homeless Assistance Center, Miami, 1999.

Right: A teddy bear sits on this well-made bed in the Alley, a makeshift but regular gathering place for homeless people in Miami, 1999.

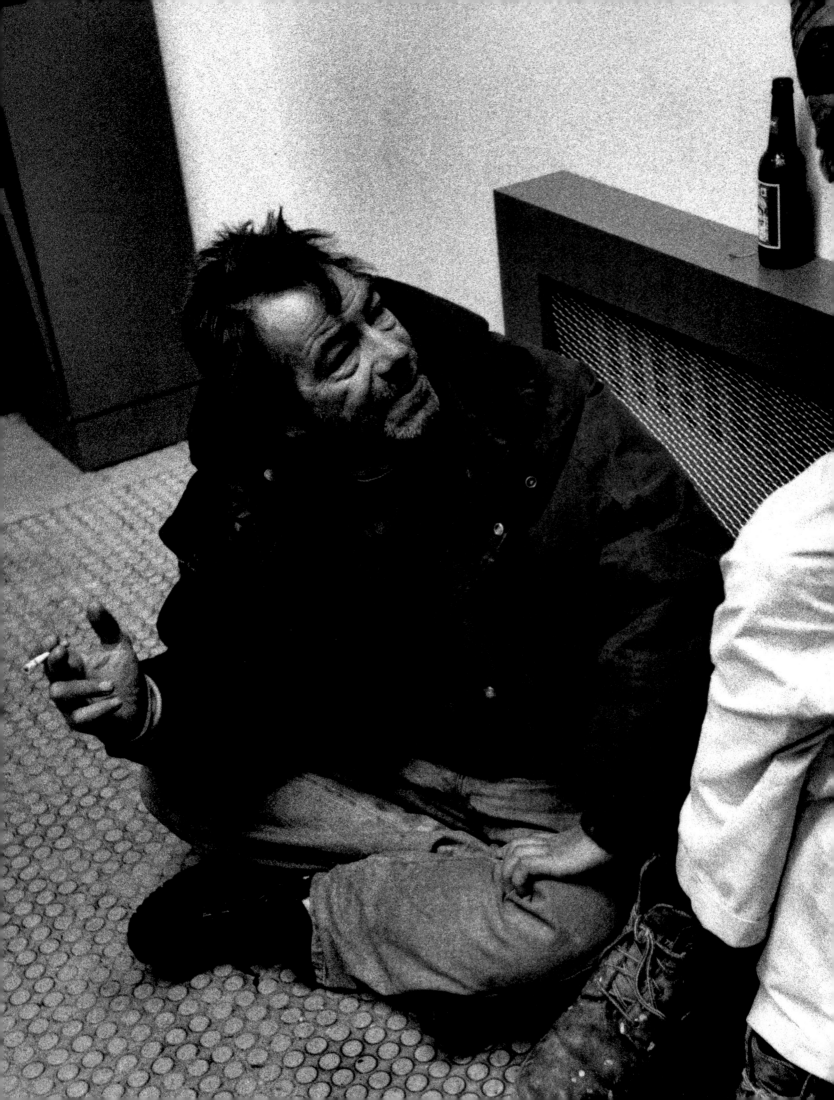

BETSY FRAMPTON

Night is when the full terror, vulnerability, and loneliness of being homeless are most fully revealed. A homeless person living on city streets finds neither peace nor privacy. To be homeless is to be always on guard, always on the move. Urban night noises—sirens, cars, other people, even scurrying rats—discombobulate the soul. What little light there is disturbs rather than soothes. Refuges such as bank automatic-teller kiosks and subway cars glare with buzzing fluorescent light, while on the street the headlights of passing vehicles and blinking traffic lights daze and disorient.

This kaleidoscope of street images at night represents my reentry to photography after a long absence. Through them I was able to revive my lifelong passion for photographing the human experience. In doing so, I have been privileged to witness a part of the journey taken by many remarkable people, both those who are homeless and those who work to help them. Their resilience, humor, and wisdom as they confront daily challenges have inspired me. I hope that some of the individuals I met and photographed have already found their way home as I have found mine.

Betsy Frampton photographed in Boston, Massachusetts, in 1999.

Night in an ATM kiosk in Boston.

Above and right: Alcoholism is only one of many health problems on the street. Every night in Boston two mobile units, each with at least one medical person and two outreach workers, patrol the streets and back alleys of the city. They bring hot food, blankets, clothing, and, most important, a sympathetic ear. This consistent and supportive approach engenders trust and encourages people who can no longer cope with living on the street to enter shelters, detoxification programs, and hospitals. One of the most respected and popular medical practitioners in this community is Dr. Jim O'Connell. He was a key player in the development of health care for homeless people in Boston in the mid-1980s. He pioneered the concept of a community health center without walls. This effective service-delivery model is predicated on multidisciplinary teams of full-time physicians, nurse practitioners, nurses, case workers, and mental-health clinicians who provide care in hospitals and shelters and on the streets.

"Perhaps," said a Boston street dweller, "if I had heard positive voices, I never would have taken a drink."

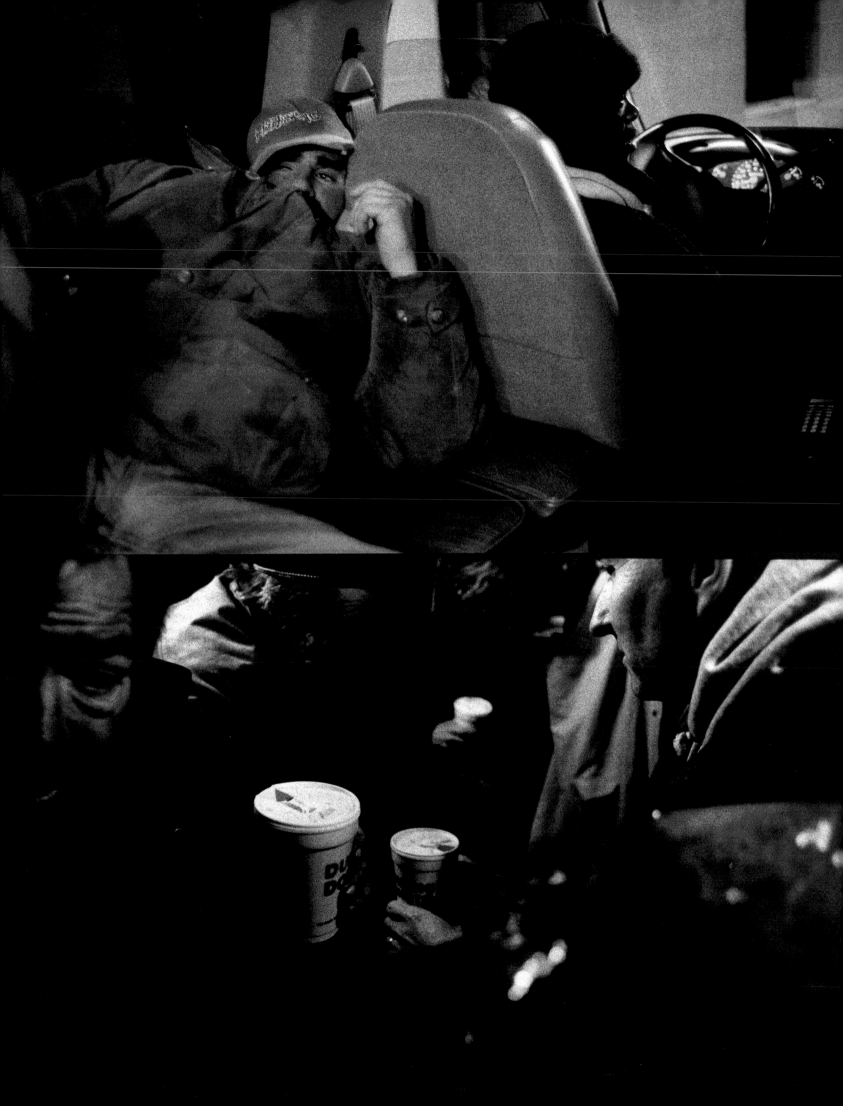

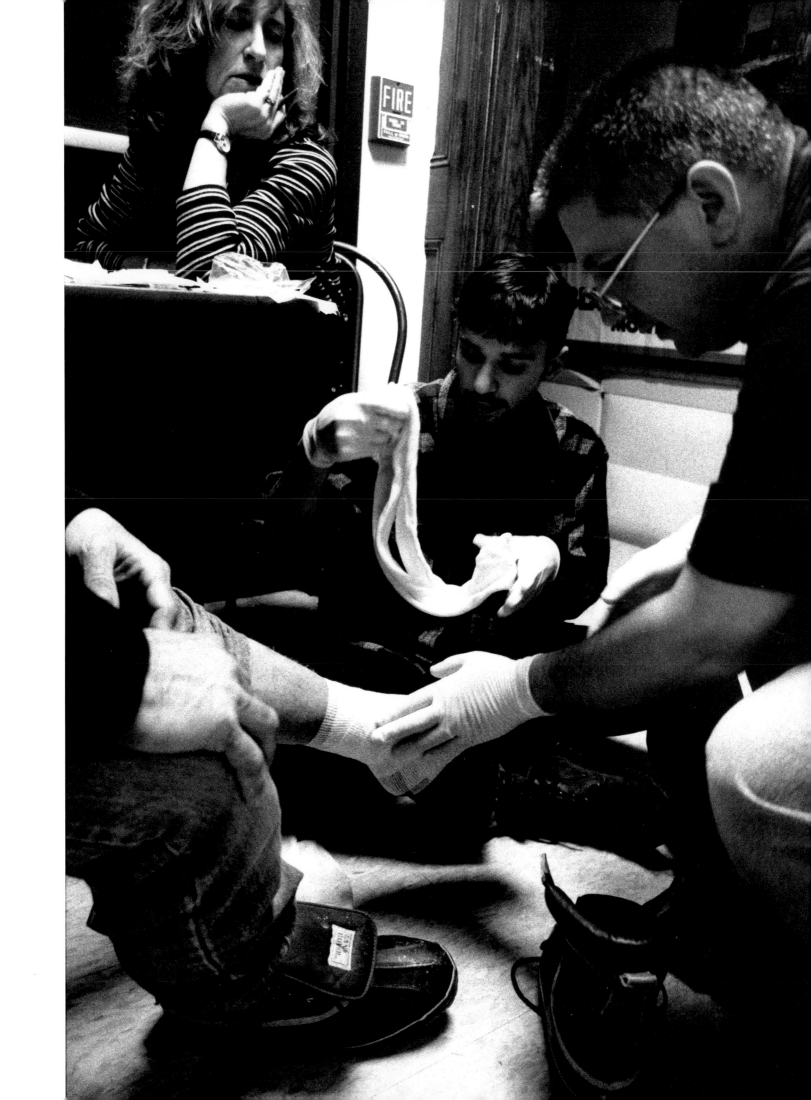

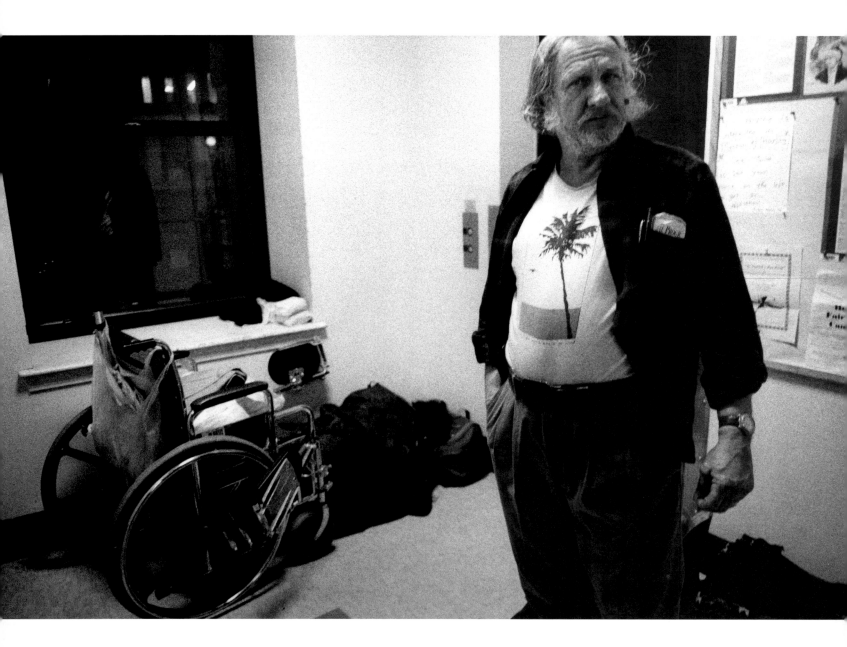

Page 80: Dianne, homeless since age 13, meticulously makes up her cot every night with her cherished blankets and pillows. During the day, she must carry around two thirty-gallon trash bags containing her bedding because she has no place to leave them when the shelter closes in the morning.

Previous page: At the Boston Night Center, Toni Abraham, a nurse practitioner from the Boston Health Care for the Homeless program, supervises while nurse Jack Castro and Mark Lepore, a student from Boston University Medical School, bandage the badly infected foot of a homeless man. Swelling of the feet and legs, cellulitis, and skin ulcerations are common among people living on the street. Inadequate opportunities to bathe, ill-fitting and wet shoes, and exposure to the elements all contribute to medical problems.

Left: As the temperature drops, Linda and Gerald reluctantly spend the night at a shelter, rather than on the streets. This emergency facility, which will admit people who are drunk, is sometimes referred to on the street as the "Nightmare Center" or "Fright Center." There are no beds, so guests must sleep on chairs or on the floor. Linda sleeps under her wheelchair because she worries that someone might steal it.

Below: When the lights go out in this small Boston shelter, men sleep on cots on one side of the room, women on the other. Tammy and Rodney try to share a tender moment, but privacy does not exist in this crowded environment.

Overleaf: Darrel and Barbara met a year ago when Darrel saw Barbara sitting on a wall. "We talked and decided to pool our money to buy a half-pint," he says. "We've been together ever since." On frigid weekends, especially after the sun sets and before the shelter opens, they ride the subway to keep warm. "Riding the train gives us some peace, some space away from the rest of them."

THE PEOPLE WHO HAD TO GO

LEE STRINGER

It had been decided, piece by piece, in whatever
nonsmoking-filled rooms, that for the sake of our city
   the gray, Terminal man,
     whose spine has him bent nearly chin to knee,
     who haunts Grand Central day after day,
     lugging bags of dead newspapers to and fro . . .
Would have to go.
And the woman there with the elephantine legs, all wrapped in
     gauze and reeking of pus, who rebukes the Skyscraper
     People at the top of her lungs
     for all having wronged her so . . .
That fat old Jane Doe—she'd have to go.

And that frizzled-haired, ragged-voiced,
rotted-teeth blond who clings to her bottle
and her big black man and laughs out too loud,
     like the scream of a crow . . .
Both him and her would have to go.

And Dumpster Divers,
Tarry and black with syrup and grime,
Digging for nickels a can at a time . . .
The Looney Tunes
now risen from their psyche-ward beds
to wander around midtown, never taking their meds . . .
They startle the good people so,
spook all the tourists who spend at the shows.

The moles,
living underground where none of us dare go . . .
The winos,
still toasting a past that was never really so . . .
And welfare moms,
left in the lurch when they started to show . . .
Old folks,
dying slowly in the windows of doomed SROs . . .
Squeegee guys
who, after they wipe, shove a palm at your nose . . .
The flat, hungry faces,
Pressed against the windows of Restaurant Row . . .
The hooked hookers,
Out to score a few bucks for their wakeup blow . . .

The artists with no walls to show,
who eat up the sidewalks of So and NoHo . . .
The peddlers
Shilling their hot swag, priced ready to go . . .

It had been decided,
by all the right people,
from all the right places,
each of some substance and all in the know,
that for the sake of this city the sick, the suffering, the strung-out,
the shifty, the lost, the lonely, the luckless, the mad, the bewildered,
the hopeless, the weary, the trapped, the dependent, the penniless,
the abandoned, the weak, the dying, the unloved . . .
These—and many more yet to come—would just have to go.

Note: These are people I recall from my days on the streets of New York, who—shortly after
"quality of life" became a political catchword there—disappeared from sight.

DONNA FERRATO

In 1999 I lived for a few days with fifty women and children at the Olive Branch Mission in Chicago. It is the most crowded residence I've ever seen, a basement with rows of bunk beds. My first night in this subterranean sanctuary was tougher than those I'd spent photographing in prison. A chorus of asthmatic, wheezing, sobbing children kept me awake, wondering how I—how anyone—can find solutions in such circumstances.

But at six the next morning a young boy with kind brown eyes stared at me, smiled, and asked if I'd slept well. This was Pierre Garrett. Over the next few days I got to know Pierre and his family. I saw the love, strict attention, and devotion that their mother, Margie, and many other mothers lavished on their children. I saw how a single mother can find solutions if she can gain access to opportunities such as job-assistance programs.

The wisest investment we can make for the future is in children and struggling mothers like Margie, who need financial aid, child-care assistance, and affordable housing. Against the odds, Margie was making a change. The safety net of basic services and counseling is an essential part of that achievement.

Donna Ferrato photographed in Chicago, Illinois, in 1999.

Boys in the shelter hug Pierre Garrett after a tearful confrontation with his mother.

87

Above: I rarely saw kids in the shelter play. Shelter life is a serious game. This baby waits anxiously for his mama to take him to bed.

Right: Margie's son, Jamont, 9, watches from his perch on a bunk bed as his mother chooses a dress for her job-training class. In the United States an alarming number of children are homeless.

HOMELESSNESS IS NOT A SIN

GREGORY C. HILL

Homelessness is not a sin
Homelessness is not a crime
It is more than just "Miss, do you have a quarter?"
Or "Sir, do you have a dime?"

Homelessness has proven to be
A valuable lesson

The innocent righteous may live
In the very same shelters
With the one
Who may carry a gun
Named after Smith and Wesson.

Homelessness may be resolved
One day

It will take the world being healed
Of selfishness and greed
It will take hearts overflowing with love
To fulfill a homeless person's needs

Compassion is required
When you look into a homeless person's face
Whoever finds it difficult to care
Should just try living
In a homeless person's place.

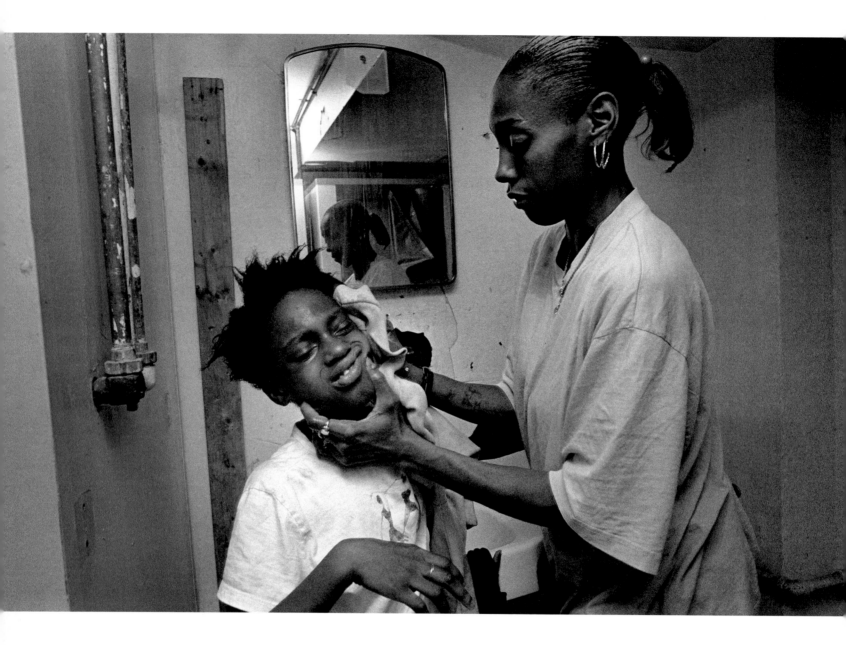

The bathroom at the mission is dreary at best, with holes in the walls and floor, peeling lead paint, no toilet paper, showers without handles. Mothers nevertheless keep their children scrupulously clean, singing praise to God. Here, Renee cleans her daughter's face with plenty of elbow grease.

All the other mothers loved Margie, who gave kids free professional haircuts every night. Hopefully, with luck and hard work, her positive attitude will take her far up and away from homelessness.

A young woman holds her baby brother high.

Standing between their bunk beds, Margie admires her four sons: Johnny, 13, Pierre, 11, Jamont, 9, Johnnell, 11. She always took care of her kids until she fell in love with a drug addict and became addicted herself. Her children's world fell apart, and they became homeless residents at the mission.

7:00 A.M.: Margie rides the train to her job-training class in downtown Chicago. Accompanying her is Cherilyn, a resident at the Olive Branch who recently found a job as a home-care worker.

Right: The Olive Branch is a dark, oppressive space, but it gets the message across to the women who stay there that the solutions to their problems are in their own hands. Ignoring distractions, Margie finishes her homework for job-training class.

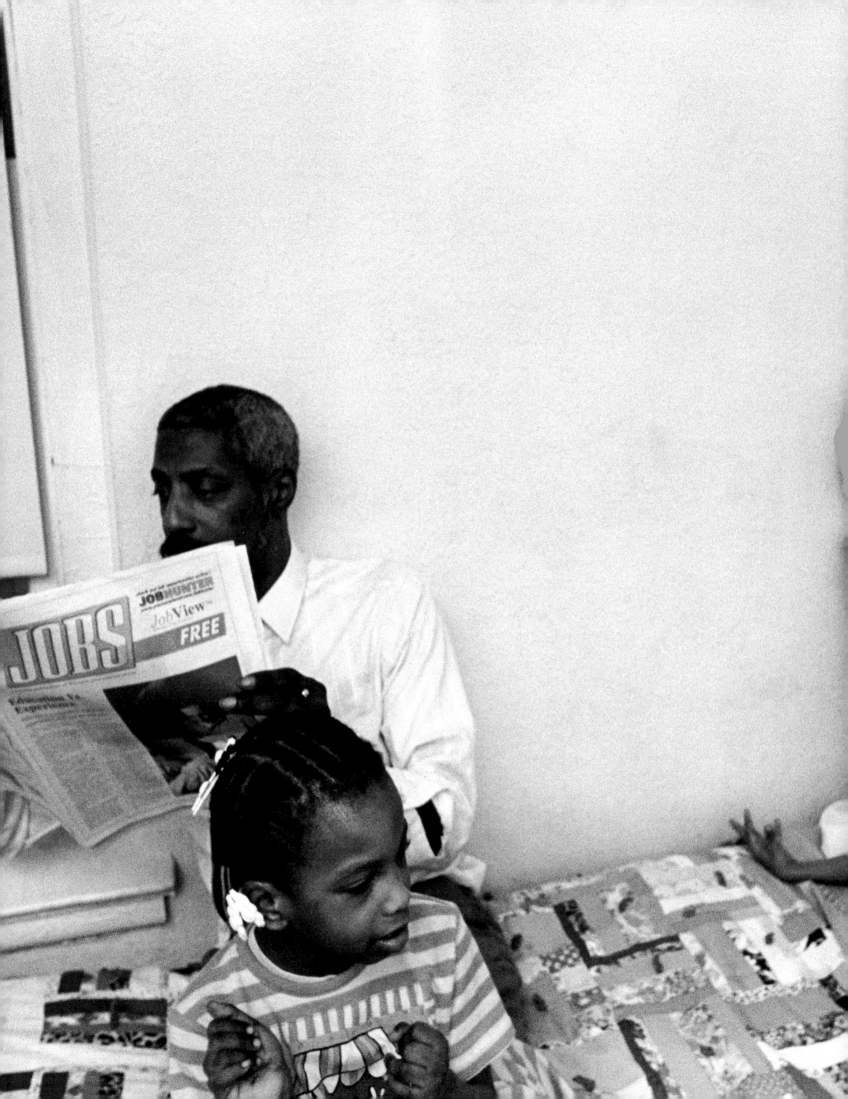

JOSEPH RODRIGUEZ

In 1999 we are in an economic boom in the United States. I heard a reporter talk about the rise in employment opportunities in Minneapolis and St. Paul and the shortage of people to fill those jobs. As a result, people were moving there in search of a better life. So I went to Minnesota to see what homelessness looks like in such circumstances. I found that jobs are available, but there is a serious shortage of affordable permanent housing. I met many people working in programs designed to end homelessness, from job-training projects to transitional housing. The Twin Cities have a large support network to help families and individuals whose dream is to make a new home there. But the basic need for inexpensive housing remains unfulfilled.

Joseph Rodriguez photographed in Minneapolis and St. Paul, Minnesota, in 1999.

At the Lowry Family Shelter in St. Paul, Don Oden looks through the classified ads as his children, Don, 6, and Stacey, 5, play. "My wife is in jail because of drugs, prostitution, and welfare fraud," he recounts, "and I have custody of my two children. I wanted to start somewhere new. I want these two kids here to have a better life, not to have to worry about drugs. My kids are stress-free and feel good. In St. Paul there's plenty of employment but not enough housing. The landlords want you to have steady employment, but I need a place for my family first; I can't leave them with strangers while I work. I have come to the Lowry shelter. I'm working on my résumé. I'm in a church group for support. It's just the housing that brings me down; otherwise, I feel positive."

Beds at the Union Gospel Mission in St. Paul are not free. If you get there early enough, you can buy one for the night. But they go fast, and by the time many working homeless people get off work the beds are all taken. There is also a lottery each night for beds and those who don't win are offered a floor mat instead.

Right: The Freeman children play in the apartment in St. Paul where they live with their mother, Lashaunda. Now the landlord is evicting them. Before they found this apartment, they moved from shelter to shelter. Annabelle Wagner, a social worker for House Calls Healthcare for the Homeless, visits Lashaunda often to check on the children. "With welfare reform many people are working, but there is not enough child care. Some families are leaving their children with undesirable people to watch over them. We are one of the few agencies that transport clients to look for jobs, medical appointments, and housing. Having a car is essential. We work mostly with single moms and their kids."

Near right: Amanda Adams, 18, with her 2-year-old daughter, Alyssa, at Elim Transitional Housing in Minneapolis. Amanda's parents were alcoholics who traveled from state to state looking for work. She was born in Iowa and was a runaway teenager. Through Elim's Teen Mother Program, young mothers can stay at the home for up to two years while earning a high-school general-equivalency diploma and finding employment. The school Amanda attends provides day care.

Far right: Navarro Mandell, 20, and Jennifer Harris, 16, in her room at the Archdale, which provides permanent housing for homeless youth in Minneapolis in collaboration with the Bridge for Runaway Youth, Inc. and the Central Community Housing Trust. Jennifer says, "I ran away from home when I was 13 because my stepfather was abusive. I stayed with friends and family until I got help through the Bridge."

Left: Lachia Jones, 22, grew up on Chicago's South Side. She had problems with her family— her mother was a drug addict— and lived with her grandparents. When she couldn't stay with them any longer, she decided to go to Minneapolis to find her aunt and cousins. She ended up in a shelter with her four children. She has found helpful programs in Minneapolis, "and it's easier to get work here," she says. Lachia is trying to get her children into school and wants to study to be a nurse's assistant. She is moving into an apartment that the people at Elim Transitional Housing helped her to find.

Right: Charles Peake, 39, looks out the window of Anishinabe Wakiangun, a long-term residence in Minneapolis for Native Americans with addiction problems. Minneapolis has the largest urban Indian community in the United States. Most of the residents here are alcoholic, single, adult, and male. Many went through the foster-care system as children. An alcoholic living on the streets costs the taxpayer between $35,000 and $40,000 a year in emergency medical services, ambulatory services, police, and detoxification programs. Anishinabe Wakiangun houses them for $15,000 a year each, which includes a room, food, medical care, and case management.

Harold Flournoy, 38, sleeps in his tent by the bank of the Mississippi River. Flournoy worked in the printing business, began using crack cocaine, and lost everything. He got off drugs and back on track after taking some technical-training courses, but found only temporary jobs as a security guard and assistant building manager. Then he fell back into drug use. "My dad was from Missouri and worked on the barges of the Mississippi River when we were small children, until he got a job as a janitor at the University of Minnesota. I like it out here in nature because I'm not around drugs. I won't go to shelters because they're not safe. I'm happy when I'm out here. I don't care about the harsh weather. It's going to be hard for me to go back and adjust to society."

Right: Ed Gist's son Andre plays outside their new apartment. Gist moved to St. Paul from St. Louis to begin a new life after their mother died. A hardworking single father, he says, "I came from a family of eight and my father taught us to take care of your family, have faith in yourself, and always try to be honest." When he first arrived in St. Paul, the Wilder Roof Transitional Housing Organization helped him find housing and work. He is employed as a nurse's assistant and wants to get his nursing degree. He has never been addicted to drugs or alcohol, or lived on the street.

GOING ON
RANDOLPH SHAIRD

You wake up like any other day,
Unaware of the total change it will bring.
Funny how you never think of
Something so natural, Death.
Like a violent, fast-moving storm,
It struck and left devastation
and unbelievable harm.
You walk around in a daze.
Time ceases to exist.
Nothing seems real.
Try to tell yourself
This is a dream, it can't be real.
Tick tock tick tock, I can't still be asleep.

Then reality rushes in, bringing with it
Unbelievable pain, surgical removal of your soul.
A piece of you has gone, but why?
What will I do? How will I do it?
What day is it? Oh God, how will I go on?
Tick tock tick tock, memories, things unsaid
Haunt you. Friends and family
Is there anything I can do? Can you bring them back?
Tick tock tick tock. Then one day you remember
The unbelievable strength the loved one had.
What would they want from me?
Oh my God, they'd want me to go on.
So go on I will. I LOVE YOU.

CALLIE SHELL

My photographs provide another view of being homeless: These people are our sisters and brothers, sons and daughters, mothers and fathers. They are teachers, artists, bus drivers, and poets. They come in all ages, shapes, and colors. They come healthy or chronically ill. They are the survivors of the street.

When we see people living on the street, we may speculate that money problems, liquor, or drugs have brought them to their present state, but they may also be fleeing physical violence or sexual abuse. Mental illness can devastate the mind, fragment the family, take away perspective, and cast a sufferer outside the safety net.

The basic needs of a homeless person are simple: a bed, a warm bath, a place to wash and store clothes, a person to talk to. Yet there comes a point when one has been alone on the streets for too long. Trust is a casualty of homelessness too.

We must help people before they reach this point. To do so, we must see them as human beings with hearts and souls. Sometimes it only takes a simple hello and a smile. Look closer, as you walk by, at that person on the corner soliciting loose change or the girl fixing her hair in the window of a shop.

Callie Shell photographed in Seattle, Washington, in 1999.

Lisa and Valerie window-shopping.

Lisa and Valerie wait in line at a Seattle referral center one evening to get a bed in a women's shelter. Lisa has an assigned bed, but Valerie must wait in this line each night until she gets one. They are both heroin addicts who are on the waiting list for a methadone-treatment program. Both are in their early twenties and from broken homes. They have had several jobs and have been in several shelters over the last year. The heroin seems to put them back on the streets. They hope that the drug-rehab program will help them get clean.

Yvonne waits across the street from the Seattle Women's Day Shelter, where she is trying to get into a drug-rehab program. She used to have her own dog. She has several children and hopes to get off the streets soon. Her children live with her mother because she does not want them to live on the street. All the rehab programs are full, with long waiting lists. During that waiting period people often fall back into a strong drug habit.

Trish Jones waits in the laundry room at Angeline's Day Shelter while her clothes are in the washer. She watches her clothes for fear of theft, but considering the backed-up schedule on the board behind her, she feels lucky to get a turn at the machine. Shelters such as Angeline's provide women with a safe place during the day to shower, wash clothes, get job referrals, and receive counseling for domestic violence or mental-health problems. Trish is washing her clothes to prepare for her job in the afternoon.

Lisa gets dressed in the morning at a Seattle overnight shelter that provides showers

Above: A First Place volunteer plays with a student, who admires his tattoo. Volunteers help provide the close engagement that these kids need. Many children spend their nights in shelters with a single parent who is fleeing an abusive relationship. In the first few months of attendance, a majority of the students show improvement in school and social skills.

Left: First Place is a Seattle school that welcomes homeless children. Debra Holland, an administrator and counselor, reads to Kim (right) and Serenity (left) in their classroom. The program provides counseling, social services, transportation, and tutoring, in addition to schooling in a safe environment. Many of the enrolled children have been abused or neglected. Teachers, counselors, and volunteers stress one-on-one attention.

Pamela, 25, gives her 5-year-old son Xzavier a kiss at bedtime at Seattle's Emergency Shelter. Pamela had been to several night shelters with her two sons, before they were able to get into this program. The shelter provides families with a temporary, sparsely furnished apartment in a safe environment. Although available for only a limited time, it has given Pamela a chance to find a job, order her finances, and enroll her children in school. She hopes to have her own apartment soon.

Georgette and her three children ran away from her abusive husband in the middle of the night and moved to another town, where her husband could not find them. They were able to get a temporary apartment in a building for single women with children. Here, Georgette listens to her youngest child, 6-year-old Torrence, read. Through a domestic-violence program, Georgette and her children have received counseling. Although terrified to start out on her own, Georgette has been able to find a job and place her kids in school. She hopes to move into her own apartment soon. At first her kids were very combative at school, but they are now all doing well. Many women will not flee an abusive relationship for fear of not being able to care for their children. Georgette is proof that they can.

STEPHEN SHAMES

These images document programs to combat homelessness. They shed light on people who are too often forgotten, particularly children. Some are not yet literally homeless, but at severe risk. They are spiritually homeless, living in families on the verge of disintegration.

In addition to maintaining emergency shelters, we must equip parents and guardians with the tools to provide even the youngest of children with emotional and physical security. That's why I believe parenting and mentoring programs are a solution to homelessness. A loving, nurturing environment should be prepared for children before they are born, for there is no greater good than bringing a child's soul into a safe harbor.

Stephen Shames photographed in El Paso, Texas, and Chicago, Illinois, in 1999.

Chicago: Steven Rudolph with his 2-year-old son, Carrio. "From the time I was a child," he recalls, "I lived life as a criminal. By the age of 8 I was drinking and drugging. I joined a gang at 9 or 10 and my life was jail. Four years ago I decided to change my life. I left my block and became homeless, which was an improvement." Eventually, Steve found living space at Lakefront SRO, a nonprofit developer of 700 single-room-occupancy units for adults. "When I got to Lakefront I was so happy. It meant something to have my name on the lease." Steve is now a Job Coach at Lakefront and is raising his son.

"He beat my mom up," explains 10-year-old Alfonso. "That's why my mom and us are here." Maria Paniagua left her home to escape domestic violence, moving from shelter to shelter with her children and saving their welfare money for rent. Her kids are American citizens, though she is not. After a week at Enunciation House, an El Paso shelter for undocumented people, they moved into their own apartment. Most residents at this shelter need temporary lodging while they catch their breath and save to reach their goals. Enunciation House is funded by private donations and staffed by volunteers.

Above: Honduran refugees staying at Enunciation House wait for people to drive by and offer them day-labor work. They came to the United States after Hurricane Mitch devastated their nation's agriculture in 1998, eliminating their livelihood.

Below: A young man telephones relatives to let them know he is coming as soon as he has money for a bus ticket.

When her mom became homeless, teenage Jennifer, pregnant and with a baby, moved in with her boyfriend. That situation grew unstable: her baby became ill and her boyfriend's emotional abuse drove her to a brief hospitalization. Jenny entered the eighteen-month Transitional Living Program of the El Paso Center for Children.

Jenny earned her high-school equivalency diploma while living at the center and working part-time. Now out of the program, she works full time in a fast-food restaurant and has her own apartment. Reaching her goals meant overcoming a mental-health crisis and having access to support, advice, and a structured program. "We got her psychological help and worked through the crisis with her," says Jeanne Hosch, director of the Transitional Living Program.

Above left: At the center, her daughter Jacinda, 2, cries; *below left:* Jennifer hugs Jacinda.

NOTE FROM A RUNAWAY GIRL
ANONYMOUS

No food
No necessities (toilet paper or shampoo)
I steal for food
I steal for clothes
I'm tired of doing drugs and being on the streets
I want a better
Life.

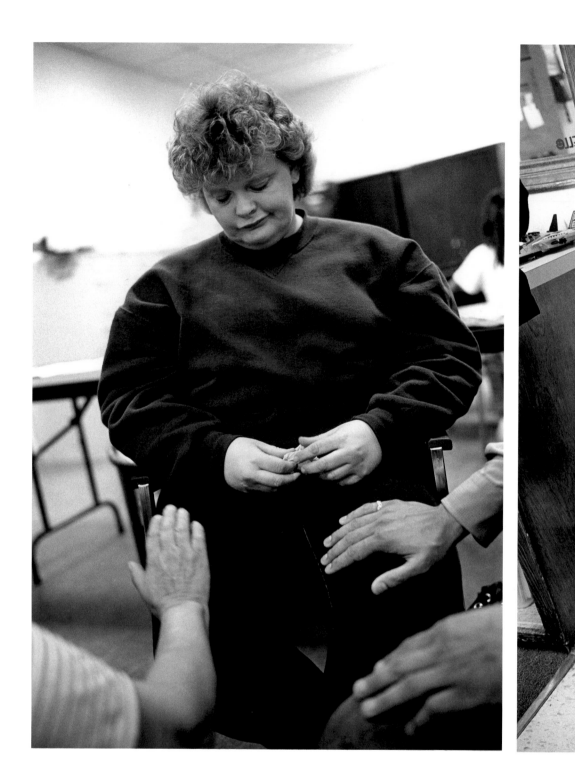

David, 11, was placed in the El Paso Child Crisis Center after he called the police and accused his stepfather of hitting him. The center provides an emergency shelter for children under 13 who are homeless because of abuse, neglect, or other family crisis. Child Protective Services investigated and found no evidence of abuse, but the episode prompted the family to seek help for David and themselves.

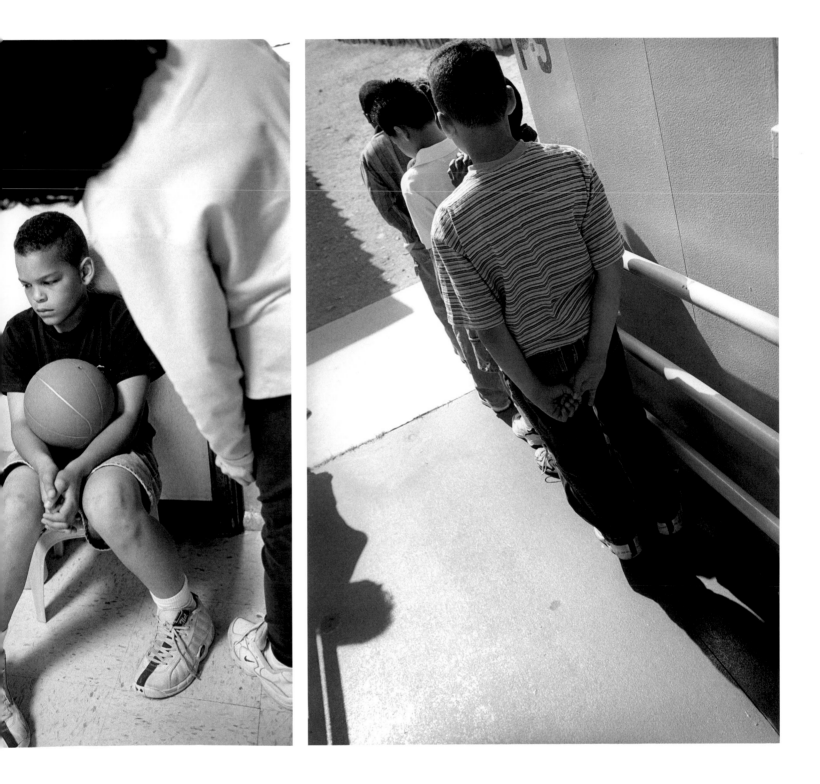

Left: David's mother, Donna, is comforted by her husband and others at a parent support-group session run by Aliviane, Inc. They also have a weekly in-home counseling session with Family Services of El Paso. *Center:* A counselor at the Crisis Center comforts David after an outburst. *Right:* David, now living at home again, attends Project About Face, an El Paso alternative elementary school.

Far left: At the El Paso Child Crisis Center, 12-year-old Chris talks to his mom as his sister Desiree, 8, watches. When their 6-year-old sister, Dominique, needed brain surgery, her mom stayed in the hospital with her. A single mother, she placed the two older children in the Center temporarily. "The Center's helped me a lot," she says. "I've been in terrible jams. They've been there for me and my kids."

Near left: A staff member plays with Chris.

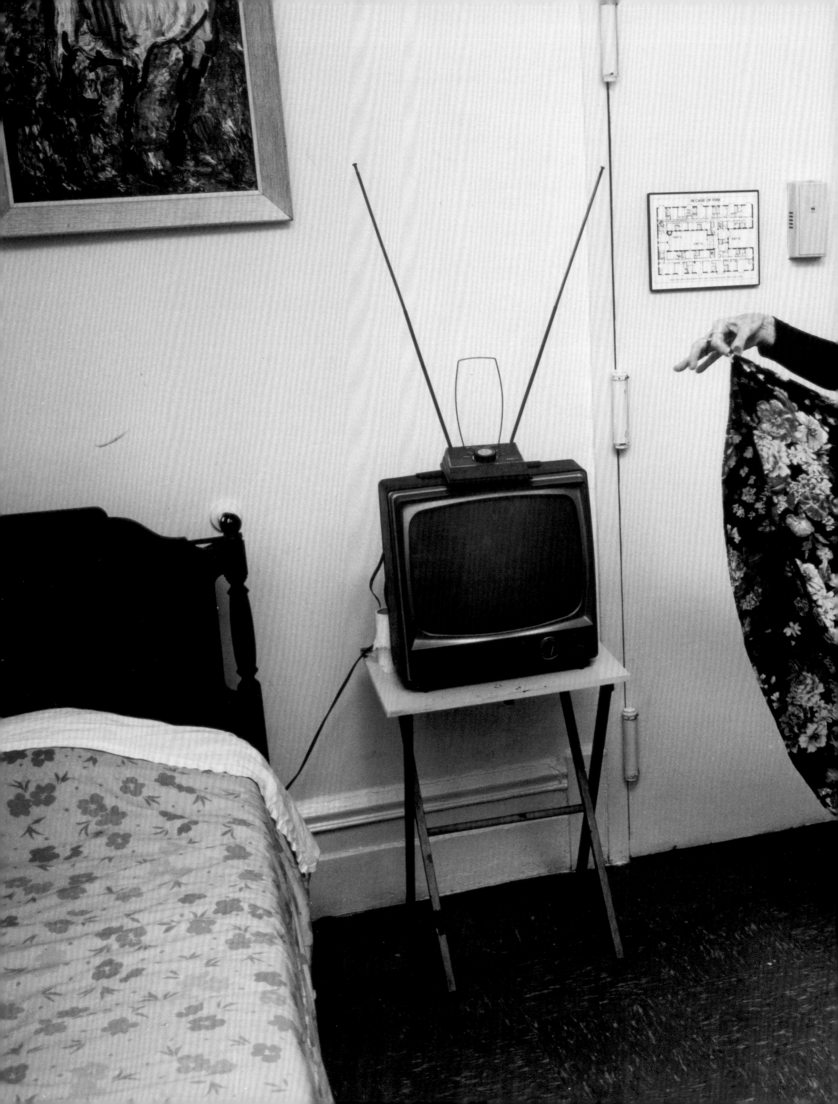

ANNIE LEIBOVITZ

The Times Square residence is an elegant historic landmark in Manhattan that houses 652 single adults, half formerly homeless and all part of a wonderful story of renewal and possibility.

The old Times Square Hotel was a notorious "welfare hotel." With loans from New York City, private investment, and federal low-income and historic-rehabilitation tax-credit programs, Common Ground and the Center for Urban Community Services purchased the derelict building and renovated it as permanent housing for homeless and low-income adults. Among the tenants are the elderly, people with AIDS, the mentally ill, recovering substance abusers, and a host of individuals simply struggling to survive in a city where housing is shockingly expensive. On-site services are integrated within the residence, including employment training and placement.

Down the street is the Woodstock Hotel, an SRO residence for low-income adults over age 55, many of whom have special needs. One of several inspiring sites managed by Project FIND, it also provides community resources: a vibrant, activity-filled senior center that serves meals; a part-time medical clinic; and a drop-in center where people can take a shower, receive clean clothes, and obtain referrals for other social services.

Annie Leibovitz photographed in New York City in 1997.

Valerie Choinacki, Woodstock Hotel.

127

Sadie Gerst, the Times Square residence.

Gloria Senger, The Times Square residence.

Jane Cassidy, the Times Square hotel.

Thereza Feliconio, Woodstock Hotel.

THERE'S NO PLACE LIKE HOME

DIANA WALKER

When I took the assignment to photograph facilities in Arlington and Baltimore, I imagined rows of cots filled with the homeless people I have become so (inexcusably) accustomed to seeing on street corners in Anywhere, USA. In the past, I allowed myself to pass on by. Now it was time for me to find out why this happens to people, what is being done to help, and what more can be done.

So off I went, much as I would on any assignment for *Time,* to document what I saw with a quiet camera and very fast film. What I found were groups of people down on their luck, fighting hard to get their lives back on track, with the help of social workers and volunteers. I was astounded both at the dedication of those working to help and those trying to help themselves, and at the goodheartedness of givers and receivers. I saw hope, I saw successes, I saw connections, I saw understanding, as well as enormous effort. We all need to understand, to lend a hand.

Diana Walker photographed in Arlington, Virginia, and Baltimore, Maryland, in 1999.

Kesha and Roger graduated from Arlington-Alexandria Coalition for the Homeless's (AACH) Adopt-A-Family program in May 1998. Today they enjoy watching their daughters play in the living room of their small apartment. They moved into their new home, built by the Habitat for Humanity program, in August 1999.

A 4-year-old boy plays with toys he received through the AACH Holiday Hook-Up Program, while his mother looks on. This program helps more than one hundred families and individuals at Christmas by providing presents and food baskets.

A mother kisses her infant son during a quiet moment together at Sullivan House, a shelter in Arlington, Virginia. Domestic violence and the child's ill health led this family to seek refuge there.

Homeless veterans often have a particular constellation of problems to overcome. A unique component of the Maryland Center for Veterans Education and Training is its structure, which is based on a military model, emphasizing individual accountability, self-discipline, organization, and teamwork. Groups of residents (troops and squads) are answerable to each other and to the designated platoon leadership. Peer pressure promotes individual responsibility for actions taken. In keeping with the military structure, all residents are required to perform work details. Between five and six hundred meals are served per day. Here, program members carry out KP duty.

The Maryland Center for Veterans Education and Training serves more than two hundred veterans daily, through four distinct programs: a day drop-in shelter; an emergency shelter; transitional housing; and eighty single-room-occupancy (SRO) apartments. A veteran can progress from homelessness to permanent housing within the same site through a continuum of housing, counseling, and job-placement services. Each resident works with a case manager to develop an Individual Service Strategy, a long-range plan for remaining drug and alcohol free. Residents also attend substance-abuse classes and Alcoholics/Narcotics Anonymous meetings.

Recreation is an important component of recovery for veterans with stress-related problems. After a long day attending classes or working, social relaxation in a calm environment helps them to release the day's stress while they learn to take one day at a time.

Above: A mother and daughter return to their apartment after doing laundry at Sullivan House, one of the programs of Arlington-Alexandria Coalition for the Homeless. It is a ten-unit, fifty-bed temporary residence. Sullivan House provides emergency and short-term transitional shelter and case-management services to Arlington families and single adults.

Above left: Two years ago Patricia and Gerald Turner were homeless. After much hard work with the Adopt-A-Family program of AACH, Pat now has a new home in which to play with her son, Darrius. The house was built by Habitat for Humanity. Adopt-A-Family is an 18- to 24-month transitional program in Arlington and Alexandria that emphasizes economic independence, self-sufficiency, and an improved quality of life for formerly homeless families.

Below left: Darrius gets last-minute instructions from Mom before going off to play in the backyard of his new house.

Overleaf: At Sullivan House, a child heads out the door on his way to an evening children's program. AACH provides a number of structured activities for children through its Support for Kids in Transition program, including medical assistance, recreational activities, reading and homework help, and weekend field trips.

ENDING HOMELESSNESS IN AMERICA

We tend to think that endemic homelessness has always been a problem in our nation, but this is not so. While it is true that there were homeless people twenty years ago, homelessness as we know it today did not exist. In the 1970s a casual observer of urban America would not have seen men and women plagued by illnesses and addictions wandering the streets, their belongings piled into shopping carts or squirreled away in the entryways of buildings. If accosted for spare change, such an observer might have assumed that the beggar was destitute or alcoholic, but not that he or she was homeless. In fact, in the 1960s and 1970s many scoffed at predictions that the destruction of thousands of units of affordable housing through urban renewal and conversion of rental units to cooperatives and condominiums would result in widespread homelessness. Sadly, these predictions came true.

The realization that widespread homelessness did not exist twenty years ago helps us see the possibility that homelessness can be ended today. Unlike poverty, to which it is closely related and which, despite our great efforts and progress, has always been with us, homelessness is not inevitable. We *can* end homelessness. Indeed, we know how to do it. Having seen the enormous toll it takes on people who are homeless and on our society as a whole, it is difficult to understand why we do not.

In order to understand how to end homelessness, we have to understand the history of homelessness in our nation, who homeless people are, why people are becoming homeless now, and the progress we have made in ending homelessness.

HOMELESSNESS HAS NOT ALWAYS BEEN WITH US

Homelessness is a problem that affects virtually every community in the nation—rural and urban, wealthy and poor, large and small. Americans from all walks of life see homelessness nearly every day, and all too many Americans experience it. Yet just twenty years ago the problem was essentially nonexistent.

There is nothing new about the presence in our neighborhoods and streets of a small number of people with no regular place to call home. Throughout the twentieth century there have been people unable or unwilling to maintain a home. Dwelling on the margins of society, these "hobos" and skid-row denizens have often been called homeless, when in fact they used intermittent income from casual labor to cobble together a flexible and shifting system of housing, and rarely sleeping in the rough. They remain, however, the stereotype of homelessness.

Historically, homelessness has manifested itself periodically, when massive social and economic upheavals uprooted large numbers of poor households. Most recently, the Great Depression of the 1930s caused homelessness among thousands of families who lost or left their homes in search of new economic opportunities. Such earlier, limited experiences of homelessness did not, however, prepare us for today's widespread national problem.

The homelessness that our nation is now experiencing is different from the dislocations and skid-row experiences of the past. People who used to live on skid row still dwell in our cities, but the economics of urban renewal and downtown redevelopment are rapidly eliminating the weekly hotels and boarding houses that once accommodated their irregular incomes. Even the availability of casual and part-time labor has diminished. As a result, these people have left skid row, dispersing widely throughout our communities and spending much more time on the streets and in temporary shelters.

Today's homelessness is not caused by a particular social or economic cataclysm, but by the basic day-to-day economic challenges faced by those living in the bottom tier of the economy. Chief among these is the shortage of affordable housing. Housing costs now absorb a staggeringly high percentage of any low-income household's earnings (assuming that they have no government housing assistance). Inexpensive housing, once widely available, is now scarce: there are twice as many households in need of homes as there are units available. Homelessness, a peripheral and highly contained problem from the 1940s through the 1970s, is now devastating and national in scope.

Although most homeless people live in urban areas, many people are surprised to learn that virtually all suburban and rural communities also experience homelessness. While many localities believe that homeless people have migrated there from other, less hospitable locales, homeless people actually tend not to move around. The majority remain in the communities in which they first became homeless.

WHO IS HOMELESS?

The National Alliance to End Homelessness estimates that 730,000 Americans are homeless on any given night—and that over the course of a year this number may reach two million. The distinction between these two figures is important, because it reveals the enormous number of people who experience homelessness over the course of time. Homelessness is a dynamic problem that affects a disturbingly large percentage of poor people; it is not, as often portrayed, a static phenomenon affecting a small number of people who have chronic troubles, such as illness. It is estimated that in the latter half of the 1980s as many as seven million people experienced homelessness. And the numbers are most alarming for vulnerable groups, especially children. During a single year in New York City and

Philadelphia, one in every ten poor children experiences homelessness. One in six poor African American children is homeless, and one in five poor African American men between the ages of 30 and 50 experiences homelessness in just one year.

The majority of homeless people are men, and most live on their own (although they frequently have families, including children, living elsewhere). The average homeless person is middle-aged; only a small number are elderly. There is a small but significant number of homeless youth, unaccompanied by any parent or guardian. African Americans are disproportionately represented in the homeless population.

Perhaps a third of homeless people are families, most often a mother and her children. Two-parent homeless families are rare; homelessness itself can be the cause of family dissolution. Women undergoing an economic crisis and unable to afford housing may give up their children to either public or family foster care to keep them from becoming homeless. A 1995 study by the National Alliance found that women who had a history of foster care were themselves more likely to place their children in foster care when threatened with homelessness.

Homeless people tend to be poorly educated. Over a third lack a high-school diploma. Not surprisingly, their incomes are far below the poverty line, around $3,000 to $4,000 per year. As many as half work, but their jobs are typically erratic. They may supplement their incomes with public benefits, most often welfare, food stamps, or disability benefits from Social Security.

Around a third of homeless people have mental illness and about the same percentage have chronic substance- or alcohol-abuse illness. It is not unusual for homeless people with mental illness and little family structure, social support, or other resources to become addicted to alcohol or drugs in an attempt to self-medicate their symptoms. Approximately a third of people who are homeless are armed-forces veterans.

Many homeless people have some history of spending time in a public institution, such as a foster-care home, a mental hospital, or a prison. The failure of these public institutions adequately to address the needs of those in their care is a major cause of homelessness. For example, many children in foster care spend years moving from one household or group home to another. When such children are released from the public system, they have learned few of the skills required to establish a stable family, employment, or housing. It is not surprising, then, to find poor outcomes for many foster-care graduates. A 1995 Alliance study found that homeless people were at least three times more likely to have been in foster care than other Americans.

Another institutional path into homelessness is prison, and sadly this may be more closely linked to mental health than to crime. Jails and prisons have become the public mental-health facilities of last resort for the very poor. Very poor mentally ill people have difficulty obtaining adequate treatment or medication; without such assistance they may engage in inappropriate public behavior. Penal institutions are ill-equipped to address the needs of people with chronic mental illness, a fact that can prolong the institutional stay of such inmates. And whether or not the inmate is ill, prisons do an inadequate job of planning the discharge of their poorest inmates. Inmates without resources or family may simply be released with a list of area shelters, creating a housing cycle of shelter, street, and prison.

These demographics and characteristics point out two common misconceptions about homelessness. The first is that we are all just a paycheck away from homelessness. Certainly it is true that anyone may become homeless. Any shelter operator can tell you the story of a homeless client who was a corporate executive or has a Ph.D. But most homeless people are not well-educated individuals fallen from the middle class, with histories of regular employment and family stability. Most are very poor people with limited earning ability, who cannot afford housing.

The second misconception is that everyone who is homeless has mental illness or abuses alcohol or drugs. While many people who are homeless do have chronic illnesses, long-term longitudinal analysis of the problem shows that the vast majority do not. They are homeless because of an immediate economic or housing crisis.

This, then, is a profile of the homeless population. For the answer to what causes homelessness we must look at how several decades of systemic economic and social changes have affected low-income Americans.

THE ABSENCE OF HOUSING

Homelessness is, by definition, the absence of housing. We have always had extreme poverty in our nation—there have always been people with mental illness, alcoholism, and a low level of education. But in the past they could find a place to live. Why is this no longer the case? The answer lies in the interaction of three elements—housing, income, and services.

America has no shortage of housing. In fact, we are probably the best-housed nation in the world. We have achieved a very high level of home ownership and have made great inroads in the elimination of substandard housing. Despite these successes, affordable housing is in short supply, and in the last thirty years has grown ever more scarce. In cities, inexpensive housing has been in part a casualty of economic revival: as cities have been transformed by urban renewal and gentrification, the traditional homes of the very poor—boarding houses and SROs (single-room-occupancy units, modest rooms available on a short-term basis to people without a steady income)—have been converted to condominiums and market-rate rentals. The private sector has no incentive to retain this affordable stock, which generates little profit. The public sector, which for many years addressed the affordable-housing shortfall with federal, state, and local subsidy programs, has instead reduced its role over the past twenty years. The resulting shortage is a prime cause of homelessness.

In addition, some household incomes are so low that they

simply do not cover basic needs, such as shelter. Over the past twenty years the average income of poor people has not kept pace with the good economy. The minimum wage has not matched inflation. Jobs in industry, in which people with low education and skill levels once earned good wages and a measure of job security, have decreased. They have been replaced by low-wage service-sector jobs with no job security. The safety net of public services to support our most vulnerable citizens is badly frayed.

Indeed, a third key cause of homelessness is lack of services. We all need and use services every day. Poor people, who have few other resources, often rely on publicly funded medical treatment, day care, legal services, job counseling, and retraining. Poor people with disabilities have need of additional assistance. When basic needs of this sort are unmet the result is ill health and economic instability, unwholesome conditions for individuals and for communities.

Thus, insufficient affordable housing, low income, and unmet service needs interact to cause homelessness. A person without stable housing finds it difficult to hold a job; someone without a job cannot afford housing. Without housing, school and services such as health care are difficult to get to and their effectiveness is diminished.

The deinstitutionalization of mentally ill people amply demonstrates the interaction among housing, income, and services. In the 1960s and 1970s newly developed medications made it possible for people with chronic mental illnesses to leave mental hospitals and live independently. At the time, the country had a good supply of low-income housing. People with mental illness often had little earning power, but most were eligible to receive Supplemental Security Income (SSI) and Social Security Disability Insurance (SSDI), and many states had general welfare programs, so that they were able to live on a low but reliable income. At the time, the hope was to provide outpatients with services and treatment monitored by a new infrastructure of community-based mental-health facilities. All the pieces—housing, income, and services—seemed to be in place, and deinstitutionalization proceeded rapidly. Unfortunately, over time the affordable housing disappeared. Few community mental-health facilities were ever established, so that treatment and monitoring were scarce. Without support, some mentally ill people found it difficult to get and keep jobs, and some became addicted to drugs or alcohol. At the same time, the bedrock protection of SSI and SSDI was undermined when these programs were restructured. Throughout America, fragile and vulnerable people with chronic mental illness became homeless in large numbers.

MYTHS OF HOMELESSNESS

What is homelessness like? If pressed, most of us would probably describe the life of a homeless person as a constant search for food and shelter; canvassing alleys and heating grates for a warm place to sleep, moving from soup kitchens to dumpsters in search of food, begging on the streets for cash to buy necessities, drugs, or liquor. Increasingly, however, homeless people live within an infrastructure of assistance agencies that at a minimum meet their basic needs, and at best work hard to end their homelessness.

Over the course of a year, most people who are homeless live in family units (usually a woman and her children), very few of whom spend any time on the street. Rather, they stay in shelters or longer-term transitional programs, interspersed with periods at the homes of friends or relatives. These families are homeless because they cannot afford housing. The hundreds—even thousands—of dollars in rent and deposits needed to obtain an apartment are far beyond their means. In addition, they have difficulty finding a landlord willing to overlook their typically poor credit records or troubled rental histories. So most get on the waiting list for government housing assistance—a wait that averages three years and is as high as seventeen years in some cities. Notwithstanding these barriers, 80 percent of families are homeless for a relatively short period of time and manage to make living arrangements of some kind within four months, either on their own or with the help of programs.

Men and women living separately from their children or a partner are called "single" homeless people; this does not refer to their marital status. Single people are more likely to live on the streets, although most spend their period of homelessness in the shelter system. The majority are homeless for only a short time, soon find a place to live, and never become homeless again. A smaller group tends to have repeated short episodes of homelessness; and a very small group of single people is chronically homeless. These latter, perhaps only 10 percent of the single homeless population and an even smaller proportion of the total homeless population, also are likely to have some sort of chronic illness. Nevertheless, they are the most visible to the general public, and have shaped our society's image of homelessness.

These men and women often spend significant amounts of time on the street, interspersed with stays at shelters and, increasingly, public hospitals, jails, and prisons. Because of their illnesses and their chronic use of a shelter system intended to be temporary, they absorb public and private resources disproportionately. They need a type of housing that combines a place to live with reliable, ongoing access to treatment and other services. This "supportive housing" is in extremely short supply.

It can be seen, then, that some people are homeless because economic factors limit their ability to find housing. Such families and singles tend to enter and escape homelessness relatively quickly and to draw on relatives, friends, and the community for help to do so. For them, the present homeless-assistance system works reasonably well as a safety net. But for others, particularly those who are chronically ill, the system is inadequate. The solution to their problems—long-term housing integrated with support services—requires trained and sufficient staffs and communities willing to accept them; such housing rarely exists in America today. Lacking better options, these people virtually live in the homeless-assistance system, with frequent stops in jails, hospitals, and treatment programs at a tremendous cost both to them and to the public coffers.

ENDING HOMELESSNESS—HOUSING FIRST

What can we do to end homelessness? Could we end it by providing everyone with a place to live? If housing is the key to ending homelessness, why do we need an extensive infrastructure of temporary accommodation and homeless services?

Increasing the stock of affordable housing and providing housing subsidies for those who need them probably would end homelessness for most people. But this is a tall order. There are over five million American households urgently in need of housing. These families and individuals are defined as having an unstable housing situation: paying over 50 percent of their income for housing or living in overcrowded or substandard housing, or both. An alarming number of households from this group become homeless every year. To end homelessness at its source we would have to address the housing needs of this entire group. This is a laudable goal, and one that the National Alliance to End Homelessness supports. The fact that it would at least double the present federal housing budget and runs counter to current political trends may explain why it has yet to be accomplished. But even if we do not immediately find the will to end the general housing crisis, there are things we can do to make progress in ending homelessness.

Absent a comprehensive national solution, various federal, state, local, and private programs have together created an assistance infrastructure that meets the needs of the majority of homeless people fairly well, although it is oversubscribed. Most people who become homeless enter the system once and do not return. Of greater concern is the plight of recurrently homeless people, who usually have a complex of interacting chronic problems— mental illness, alcohol or substance-abuse illness, AIDS and other medical difficulties, a dearth of family members able to help—which must be addressed together. Estimates of the size of this group vary, but they are probably no more than 300,000 and possibly as few as 100,000 nationwide.

To date, the alternative to community-based supportive housing has been neglect, and this is costly for our society in every sense, human and economic. Lacking treatment, chronically ill homeless people are regularly—and increasingly—institutionalized in public facilities not designed to meet their needs: primarily jails and hospitals. The price per capita of maintaining a man or woman in jail is higher than the cost of supportive housing.

The provision of supportive housing with access to psychiatric and social-work staffs and counseling, job-training, and medical programs would free up the existing homeless-assistance system to fulfill the task it was designed for: meeting the emergency needs of those in a temporary economic crisis. Indeed, experience has shown that supportive-housing units of this kind can be successfully integrated into neighborhoods and communities, without the disruption that many may fear.

We must not dismiss the difficulties faced by low-wage households and people unable to work. A further step toward ending homelessness within the boundaries of current resources is to assess exactly what is needed to get people in an economic crisis into housing as cost-effectively as possible, and to keep them housed. We must focus on getting people into homes promptly and then linking them to the appropriate services to increase their chances of achieving long-term self-sufficiency.

Finally, we must look much more carefully at the human, social, and economic savings of preventing homelessness. At the simplest level, more could be done locally to help people stay in existing housing by preventing eviction (providing subsidized rent or utility payments, negotiating with landlords, and so on), stabilizing shared housing situations, facilitating rapid rehousing for those who lose their homes, and the like. On a more systemic level, it would be wise to give greater attention to the systems that feed homelessness. The public foster-care, criminal-justice, health, and mental-health systems routinely discharge their wards without adequate housing plans and with insufficient resources to achieve housing stability. Indeed, they are given incentives to avoid addressing the needs of those who face the most significant challenges by shifting the responsibility for these people to the emergency homeless-assistance system. Better discharge planning from these systems is urgently needed and would certainly reduce homelessness. Finally, by plotting the last addresses of homeless people we can identify neighborhoods that have a high risk of homelessness and concentrate our limited prevention resources where they will do the most good. It is cost-effective to help people avoid the debilitating and devastating condition of homelessness. Above all, it is the responsibility of a civil society to give its most vulnerable citizens shelter.

Homelessness is a problem that is both simple and complex: simple because, by definition, it is merely a lack of housing; complex because housing is expensive and difficult to provide, and because the ability of a person to find and maintain a home also depends upon his or her income and need for services.

Although it is a complicated problem, it is not insurmountably immense or monolithic. Unlike poverty, which it mirrors in many ways, it has not always been with us, nor is it inevitable. If we take the time to learn that homeless people may not be quite who we thought they were; and if we break the problem into manageable components, tailored to the needs of diverse individuals, progress can be made. Much of what we are doing to end homelessness is right. If we bring these efforts to scale and fine-tune our approach, the solution is within our grasp.

Nan Roman
President, National Alliance
to End Homelessness

KEYS TO ENDING HOMELESSNESS

The National Alliance to End Homelessness (NAEH) is a Washington, D.C.–based nonprofit organization dedicated to the principle that no American should have to be homeless. By directing the nation's largest coalition of nonprofit agencies, public-sector organizations, and corporations addressing the continuing crisis of homelessness in America, the Alliance advances practical, realistic, community-based solutions in programs, policy, and public education.

There are many effective ways by which individuals and groups can and do take firm steps toward ending homelessness each day. Here are some suggestions for how you can channel your own energy and talents in joining the cause:

EDUCATE . . . yourself, your family, your friends, your colleagues, and your community on the causes of homelessness, statistics about it, and solutions to it. Share books, videos, and websites—and conversations with people who work in the field.

ADVOCATE . . . for policies and programs that effectively serve homeless people on the local, state, and federal levels. Support plans to create more affordable housing. Discuss current issues with housing and homeless advocacy groups. Share your concerns with public officials—tell them that you want homelessness to be ended. These are valuable methods of focusing community attention on solutions to homelessness.

ASK . . . your neighborhood's agencies and organizations for information about what they need. When you donate goods and services, be sure to ask what items will be most useful. Needs vary from season to season and from program to program; the familiar general categories of donations are not always the most useful gift. Consider giving clothing suitable for a job interview, home furnishings that will help a family make the transition into permanent housing, age-appropriate learning materials for children entering the local school system. Most sites have a "wish list" of the things they need most urgently. Encourage your family and community to help make those wishes come true.

VOLUNTEER . . . your time and ideas to programs within your community—and beyond. You can help to:
• plan activities for homeless families and children
• train homeless individuals for employment
• work at a nearby housing organization
• register homeless people to vote
• organize fundraising drives for local service agencies
• teach music, art, and other hobbies
• work at a shelter
• recruit others to join your efforts and to think of other creative projects.

Your skills and enthusiasm are welcome!

For more information on homelessness and how you can help, please contact:

The National Alliance to End Homelessness
1518 K Street, NW, Suite 206
Washington, DC 20005
phone: (202) 638-1526 fax: (202) 638-4664
e-mail: naeh@naeh.org
website: www.endhomelessness.org

ABOUT THE PROGRAMS

Ending homelessness is a multifaceted challenge, as is reflected by the wide variety of agencies and organizations serving the needs of homeless people around the nation. Outreach programs and emergency shelters respond to urgent and immediate problems, while other agencies build, renovate, and maintain supportive transitional and permanent housing, and still others advocate for legislative action and funding. Many sites offer counseling, medical clinics, and educational programs, and a great number of organizations provide a spectrum of these services, plus housing, under one umbrella. Some focus on the needs of families, others on those of children, the elderly, veterans, AIDS patients, the mentally ill, or other groups. These are the organizations that participated in the making of this book:

CALIFORNIA

BEYOND SHELTER
3255 Wilshire Boulevard, Suite 902
Los Angeles, CA 90010
(213) 252-0772
Founded 1989
Beyond Shelter focuses on aiding homeless families. To combat the growing numbers of these in Los Angeles, it pioneered its core program, Housing First for Homeless Families, which helps such families move into affordable rental housing in residential neighborhoods, and then provides up to one year of individualized supportive services to assist the transition to stability and independence.

CONARD HOUSE
149 Ninth Street
San Francisco, CA 94103
(415) 864-7833
Founded 1959
Conard House helps adults with severe and persistent mental illness rebuild their lives after hospitalization, institutionalization, and homelessness. Its continuum of mental-health services includes counseling, case management, income advocacy, and supportive housing in 6 hotels, 16 co-op apartments, and 1 residential treatment facility. For employment training of interested clients, Conard also operates two self-sustaining food-service and catering businesses marketing to office workers in the financial and South of Market districts of San Francisco.

HOMELESS HEALTH CARE LOS ANGELES
1010 South Flower Street, 5th Floor
Los Angeles, CA 90015
(213) 744-0724
Founded 1985
Established to meet the growing health-care needs of homeless individuals and families in Los Angeles, Homeless Health Care Los Angeles and its multicultural, multidisciplinary staff use a comprehensive case-management model to provide successful drug treatment and health assistance. Client services include case management; individual and group counseling; on-site physical examinations; screening, education, and testing for tuberculosis, HIV, and STD;

preventive and acute care; dental referrals; general wellness education; and acupuncture treatment. HHCLA also offers training for other community-based organizations serving homeless and low-income people, and generates overall public awareness of homeless health-care issues through its advocacy activities.

MERCY CHARITIES HOUSING CALIFORNIA
1028-A Howard Street
San Francisco, CA 94103
(415) 487-6825
Founded 1988
Mercy Charities creates and manages communities of affordable housing and support services for poor individuals and families.

SINGLE ROOM OCCUPANCY HOUSING CORPORATION (LOS ANGELES, CA)
354 South Spring Street, Suite 400
Los Angeles, CA 90013
(213) 229-9640
Founded 1984
SRO Housing is the largest developer of its kind in the western United States, managing 16 residential hotels with over 1,400 units of permanent, supportive, transitional, and emergency housing. It also provides employment training and opportunities, rental assistance, substance-abuse recovery activities, and neighborhood park centers, all designed to revitalize Los Angeles's Central City East "Skid Row" district.

FLORIDA

DOUGLAS GARDENS COMMUNITY MENTAL HEALTH CENTER OF MIAMI BEACH, INC. (MAYFAIR RESIDENCE)
701 Lincoln Road
Miami Beach, FL 33139
(305) 531-5341
Founded 1979
Douglas Gardens provides transitional and permanent housing and supportive services in Miami Beach to current and formerly homeless individuals, through case management, crisis intervention, partial hospitalization, and/or residential treatment facilities.

HOMELESS ASSISTANCE CENTER
1550 North Miami Avenue
Miami, FL 33136
Founded 1995
The Center provides homeless individuals and families with shelter, food, clothing, showers, counseling, job training, and access to adult and vocational classrooms and primary health-care clinics. Special services such as legal aid, veteran's support programs, child care, and assistance with social security are also available, and the Center helps each guest to develop a personal case plan.

MIAMI-DADE COUNTY HOMELESS TRUST
111 Northwest 1st Street, Suite 2710
Miami, FL 33128
(305) 375-1490
Founded 1993

The Trust is responsible for implementing the Dade County Community Homeless Plan, a continuum-of-care model for housing and services for homeless people. It administers the proceeds of the county 1-percent food and beverage tax for homeless programs, and other sources of public funding; and serves in an advisory capacity to the Board of County Commissioners on all issues relating to homelessness. With 27 volunteer board members, the Trust represents the business, religious, educational, service-provider, and formerly homeless communities of greater Miami.

GEORGIA

JERUSALEM HOUSE
100 Edgewood Avenue, Suite 1228
Atlanta, GA 30303-3062
(404) 527-7627
Founded 1988
Jerusalem House manages two supportive housing facilities designed specifically for people with HIV/AIDS—one for single men and women and the other, a 2.35-acre campus, for single mothers and their children; this is the first program of its kind in Georgia.

ILLINOIS

CHICAGO COALITION FOR THE HOMELESS
1325 South Wabash Avenue, Suite 205
Chicago, IL 60605-2504
(312) 435-4548
Founded 1980
The Chicago Coalition for the Homeless conducts research and implements programs to increase the amount of available affordable housing, create jobs that pay a living wage, organize funding and opportunities for youth, and empower homeless individuals and families as voters, participants in local school systems, and respected citizens. Its area of focus is metropolitan Chicago.

LAKEFRONT SRO
4946 North Sheridan Road
Chicago, IL 60640
(773) 561-0900
Founded 1986
Lakefront SRO develops and provides affordable, supportive housing throughout Chicago. It currently operates 7 single-room-occupancy apartment buildings that provide nearly 700 men and women with comprehensive social services, job-skills training, and substance addiction recovery support. Lakefront's consulting services also encourage other organizations across the country to develop supportive housing.

OLIVE BRANCH MISSION
6310 South Claremont
Chicago, IL 60636
(773) 476-6200
Founded 1873
The oldest rescue mission in Chicago and the second oldest in the United States, Olive Branch provides emergency shelter and services to homeless and very

low-income women and children, with the goal of developing each guest's sense of independence and ability to succeed.

CENTER FOR POVERTY SOLUTIONS

2521 North Charles Street
Baltimore, MD 21218-4635
(410) 366-0600
Founded 1998
Created by a merger of the Maryland Food Committee and Action for the Homeless, the Center offers a wide range of services, including school-based health-education programs for children, families, and communities; WIC (the Women, Infants, and Children federal supplemental nutrition program); New Horizons Academy Camps for homeless and disadvantaged children; an Opportunity Fair that provides access to legal, employment, educational, medical, dental, and other services; and Baltimore Grows, which works to provide affordable, locally grown produce for low-income communities. Its mandate is to eliminate the root causes of poverty through public policy, education, research, direct-service programs, and community mobilization.

MARYLAND CENTER FOR VETERANS EDUCATION AND TRAINING

301 North High Street
Baltimore, MD 21202-4815
(410) 576-9626
Founded 1993
Founded by and for veterans, MCVET provides a day drop-in facility, emergency housing, individual counseling, transitional services, assistance for physical and mental health issues, (including post-traumatic stress disorder), job training and placement, housing placement, and general outreach. It honors the philosophy that veterans can best understand and assist fellow veterans in times of need.

BOSTON HEALTH CARE FOR THE HOMELESS PROGRAM

729 Massachusetts Avenue
Boston, MA 02118
(617) 414-3829
Founded 1985
BHCHP gives homeless people access to the same primary health-care services available to insured Bostonians. It offers regular direct-care services at over 40 sites; short-term recuperative care at Barbara McInnis House; comprehensive dental services; family and perinatal programs; HIV/AIDS services; inpatient rounds; and maintenance of individual medical records.

BREAD AND JAMS, INC.

1151 Massachusetts Avenue
Cambridge, MA 02138
(617) 441-3831
Founded 1990
Bread and Jams is a daytime drop-in center, offering showers, clothes, food, and a safe place to rest for homeless and very low-income individuals in the Cambridge area. The organization also provides assistance with housing and employment searches and encourages its clients to become more confident, independent self-help advocates. Through the national program Project Connect Bread and Jams offers voicemail to clients for jobs, health care, and other reasons.

MASSACHUSETTS HOUSING AND SHELTER ALLIANCE

Five Park Street
Boston, MA 02108
(617) 367-6447
Founded 1988
MHSA is a statewide public-policy, advocacy, and planning coalition of nearly 70 organizations that seeks the abolition of homelessness through the expansion of permanent housing, transitional programs, emergency shelter, outreach services, and economic development initiatives. It also encourages homeless self-advocacy.

PINE STREET INN

444 Harrison Avenue
Boston, MA 02118-2404
(607) 482-4944
Founded 1969
The largest shelter for homeless men and women in New England, Pine Street Inn also operates at 24 locations throughout greater Boston, offering services such as transitional housing, literacy training, tutoring in English as a second language, medical services, instruction in culinary skills, a mobile outreach van, the nightly drop-in Boston Night Center, daily activities for mentally ill guests, two thrift stores that provide job training and convert used clothing and housewares donations into revenue, and Celeste House, a facility for mothers and their children.

AMHERST H. WILDER FOUNDATION, ROOF PROJECT

Community Social Services
1600 University Avenue, Suite 219
St. Paul, MN 55104
(651) 917-6210
Founded 1995
Formed by a coalition of several private and public organizations, including the Wilder Foundation, the ROOF Project provides homeless two-parent families, single parents, large families, individuals with criminal histories, and teenage mothers in Ramsey County with temporary housing and supportive services, helping participants gain the skills necessary eventually to acquire and maintain permanent housing.

ANISHINABE WAKIANGUN

1600 East 19th Street
Minneapolis, MN 55404
(612) 871-2883
Founded 1996
Wakiangun is a long-term residential facility primarily for Native Americans in the late stages of chronic alcoholism. Three meals a day are provided, as well as other special services.

BRIDGE FOR RUNAWAY YOUTH, INC.

2200 Emerson Avenue South
Minneapolis, MN 55405
(612) 377-8800
Founded 1971
Bridge, a shelter for runaway and homeless boys and girls ages 10 to 17, provides emergency services, transitional-living services, and an aftercare program where youth who have left the Bridge may return for assistance.

CATHOLIC CHARITIES LOWRY FAMILY SHELTER

345 North Wabasha
St. Paul, MN 55102
(651) 228-0114
Founded 1991
An emergency shelter serving homeless single women and one- or two-parent families, Lowry offers three meals a day, laundry facilities, housing-advocacy services, a health team, and assistance in enrolling children in St. Paul's public schools.

CENTRAL COMMUNITY HOUSING TRUST

505 East Grant Street
Minneapolis, MN 55404
(612) 341-3148
Founded 1986
CCHT provides affordable housing and supportive services to the Loring Park, Elliot Park, North Loop, Stevens Square, and downtown areas of Minneapolis, focusing its programs on homeless youth and adults, individuals seeking counseling for substance abuse, and very low-income singles and families.

ELIM TRANSITIONAL HOUSING, INC.

3989 Central Avenue, NE, Suite 565
Minneapolis, MN 55421-3972
(612) 788-1546
Founded 1985
Elim provides affordable transitional-housing options and support services to individuals and families who are currently homeless, living in substandard housing, or living in abusive conditions. Housing is provided primarily in North and Northeast Minneapolis and in suburban Hennepin, Anoka, and Ramsey counties, and offers the opportunity for residents to live independently and pursue self-chosen goals related to stability and self-reliance.

MINNESOTA COALITION FOR THE HOMELESS

122 West Franklin Avenue, Suite 5
Minneapolis, MN 55404
(612) 870-7073
Founded 1984
The Minnesota Coalition manages the only statewide homelessness-prevention program leveraging local efforts to provide housing and services. Through its efforts in legislative advocacy, technical assistance, education, research, and data collection, the Coalition informs the public about the causes of homelessness and the ways each person can take responsibility for ending the problem.

ST. PATRICK CENTER

1200 N. Sixth Street
St. Louis, MO 63106
(314) 621-1283
Founded 1983
Established by Catholic Charities of St. Louis and now the largest provider of homeless services in the St. Louis area, St. Patrick Center currently manages 15 programs that together form a continuum of services, ranging from street outreach, mental-health stabilization, and hot meals to education, employment, and permanent housing. Among the programs offered are a 12-step drug and alcohol recovery program; the largest job-placement service in the country; a living-skills program; evening aftercare for stabilized clients successfully placed in housing and/or employment; McMurphy's Grill, the nation's first full-service restaurant for training homeless mentally ill clients;

Rosati Center, a homeless mental-health residential care facility; BEST (Building Employment Skills for Tomorrow), work training for recovering substance abusers; and Operation Independence Housing, a subsidized-housing program for homeless families who move into market-rate homes.

HELP (HOUSING ENTERPRISE FOR THE LESS PRIVILEGED) USA
30 East 33rd Street
New York, NY 10016
(212) 779-3350
Founded 1986
While its headquarters is based in New York City, HELP USA has locations across the country offering case management, supportive housing, medical and dental care, employment and life-skills training, a mentoring program for children in grades kindergarten through 8th grade, General Equivalency Degree classes, counseling for victims of domestic violence, food pantries, and much more.

THE TIMES SQUARE
Common Ground Community HDFC, Inc. and the Center for Urban Community Services
255 West 43rd Street
New York, NY 10036
(212) 768-8989
Founded 1990
With 652 efficiency apartments, on-site social and medical services, and an extensive job-training and economic-development program, the Times Square is the largest supportive-housing facility in the nation. It is sponsored by Common Ground Community. This multifaceted residence houses single adults, a population that includes formerly homeless individuals, people with AIDS, those with chronic mental illnesses, the elderly, and nearly 300 actors, musicians, sanitation workers, and other low-income working people. Many residents find employment at the on-site public venues operated by Common Ground: the Ben & Jerry's Partnershop, an ice-cream parlor, and the Top of the Times, a rooftop dining and catering facility, or at the other food businesses that occupy commercial space at the Times Square, including a Starbucks coffee shop and Daily Soup, a luncheonette.

WOODSTOCK HOTEL
127 West 43rd Street
New York, NY 10036
(212) 730-1442
Founded 1979
A single-room-occupancy hotel for formerly homeless and other low-income adults age 55 and older, Woodstock also operates a part-time medical clinic, a homeless drop-in center providing showers, clean clothing, and referrals for social services, and a senior center offering meals and a wide variety of activities. The hotel is one of three residential buildings managed by New York's Project FIND.

OUTSIDE IN
1236 Southwest Salmon Street
Portland, OR 97205
(503) 223-4121
Founded 1968
With the goal of enabling youths under age 21 to work toward self-sufficiency and healthier lives, Outside In provides an emergency drop-in center with counseling, primary and mental-health care, recreational activities, and substance-abuse referrals. The program also offers case management, developing individualized plans with clients that set personal goals for education, employment, health, and safety; an employment resource center where youths learn to obtain jobs and maintain a positive work history; and transitional housing in scattered-site apartments. Outside In also addresses the special needs of youths with HIV/AIDS, offering anonymous HIV testing, the VOICES support and education group for sexual minorities, the Streetwise peer street-outreach program, and the Gorilla Theater, which educates Portland's homeless youth about HIV and other street-life issues through a popular theater-arts format.

COALITION FOR THE HOMELESS OF HOUSTON/HARRIS COUNTY, INC.
1021 Main, Suite 1830
Houston, TX 77002
(713) 739-7514
Founded 1982
The Coalition advocates for increased governmental and private resources to meet the needs of the greater Houston homeless population. It addresses both emergency and long-term solutions in a number of ways, sponsoring the innovative Homeless Services Coordinating Council. This comprises 230 member agencies and individuals, including homeless service providers; local, state, and federal governments; community-based organizations; foundations; students; and volunteers. The Council offers technical assistance, homeless-needs assessment, and direct services.

EL PASO CENTER FOR CHILDREN
3700 Altura
El Paso, TX 79930
(915) 565-8361
Founded 1987
An emergency shelter and service facility for homeless and troubled youth, the Center offers individual and group counseling for children ages 7 through 17, overnight accommodations for those ages 10 through 17, a youth hotline, and other services.

EL PASO CHILD CRISIS CENTER
2100 North Stevens
El Paso, TX 79930
(915) 562-7955
Founded 1985
Newborn babies to children age 12 are given emergency shelter at the Center when their parents or guardians need to be alone to address personal crises and have nowhere else to turn for support in the care of their children. Parenting classes are available, as are programs for children with special needs and a structure for monitored visitation.

EL PASO COALITION FOR THE HOMELESS
1208 Myrtle Avenue
El Paso, TX 79901
(915) 577-0069
Founded 1991
The El Paso Coalition is a network of 77 entities comprising nonprofit and government agencies, churches, and individuals, designed to coordinate programs providing social services, academic classes, and employment training creating a system of comprehensive support for the homeless population of El Paso.

ENUNCIATION HOUSE
1003 East San Antonio Avenue
El Paso, TX 79901
(915) 545-4509
Founded 1978
An emergency shelter primarily serving immigrants from Mexico and Central America, Enunciation House is often the first place individuals go upon crossing the United States border. Each guest receives one-on-one attention and access to basic medical care, showers, food, clothes, tutoring in English, health education, and referrals to other programs and services. Enunciation also organizes social activities.

SEARCH
2505 Fannin
Houston, TX 77002
(713) 739-7752
Founded 1989
SEARCH's comprehensive continuum of care is represented by six main programs: a full-service day shelter/resource center and mobile outreach unit; an employment education center; the House of Tiny Treasures (the first licensed child-care facility in Houston/Harris County that exclusively serves homeless children); a medical-support program; supportive permanent and transitional on-site housing; and scattered-site affordable housing.

STAR OF HOPE
6897 Ardmore
Houston, TX 77054
(713) 748-0700
Founded 1907
The first and largest Christian mission of its kind in Houston, Star of Hope began as a men's emergency shelter and has since grown to include an emergency shelter for women and families and a transitional living center for singles and families.

ARLINGTON-ALEXANDRIA COALITION FOR THE HOMELESS, INC.
3103 Ninth Road, North
Arlington, VA 22201
(703) 525-7177
Founded 1985
AACH directs several programs that assist people toward permanent self-sufficiency and independence: the emergency and short-term transitional Sullivan House shelter; the Adopt-a-Family post-shelter transitional-assistance program; the Homeless Prevention program; Lifeworks, an employment-counseling and career-advancement service; SKIT (Support for Kids in Transition); and the Homeless Income Tax service. The Coalition thus provides services that range from preventing homelessness before it happens to providing post-shelter transitional support.

ANGELINE'S DAY CENTER FOR HOMELESS WOMEN
2025 Third Avenue
Seattle, WA 98121
(206) 461-4561
Founded 1987
A drop-in day center for homeless single women age 18 and over, Angeline's provides a place to rest, do laundry, take showers, and learn how to meet other needs such as finding permanent housing. The Center offers breakfast, lunch, and afternoon snacks, plus

mental-health counseling, crisis management, a part-time nurse, and hygiene kits.

FIRST PLACE
P.O. Box 22536
Seattle, WA 98122-0536
(206) 323-6715
Founded 1989
First Place is Seattle's school and social-service agency for homeless children and families, with programs that emphasize children's basic needs, provide social services that help to stabilize the families, and offer classroom education for boys and girls (kindergarten through 6th grade) who have been referred by local shelters, churches, and other groups.

SEATTLE EMERGENCY HOUSING SERVICE
905 Spruce Street, Suite 111
Seattle, WA 98104
(206) 461-3660
Founded 1972
One of the first agencies in the nation to provide emergency housing specifically for families, SEHS has grown to offer transitional housing; a food bank; clothing; housewares; transportation assistance; mental-health, alcohol and substance-abuse counseling; employment services; legal aid; and a preschool and day care. Since 70 percent of the individuals living in its housing units are children, SEHS has developed a special Youth Program that organizes after-school and full-day summer educational and recreational activities for children ages 6 through 17.

YWCA OF SEATTLE-KING COUNTY-SNOHOMISH COUNTY
1118 Fifth Avenue
Seattle, WA 98101
(206) 461-4851
Founded 1894
In keeping with the universal mission of the YWCA, the Seattle-King County-Snohomish County chapter works with over 20 area locations to provide women, children, and families with programs focusing on affordable housing, emergency shelter, youth development, domestic-violence services, employment services, child care, violence prevention, needs of senior citizens, and health promotion.

WASHINGTON, D.C.

MIRIAM'S KITCHEN
2401 Virginia Avenue, NW
Washington, DC 20037
(202) 452-8926
Founded 1983
Miriam's Kitchen, in downtown Washington, serves a daily hot breakfast to homeless men and women; offers access to a social worker and legal assistance; provides a mailing address and voicemail for homeless individuals; maintains a street-outreach program and veterans'-support contacts; hosts Alcoholics Anonymous meetings; and runs Miriam's Closet, which donates essential and job-interview clothing and hygiene kits. The Kitchen also conducts a visual-arts program and Miriam's Writers' Forum, a creative-writing workshop where homeless writers take part in group discussions, publish their work, and perform public readings.

ABOUT THE PHOTOGRAPHERS

JODI COBB was born in Auburn, Alabama and grew up in Iran. She received bachelor of journalism and master of arts degrees from the University of Missouri School of Journalism. She has been a staff photographer for *National Geographic* magazine since 1977, working extensively in the Middle East and Asia. Her work has been exhibited at the International Center of Photography, New York, and the Corcoran Gallery of Art, Washington, D.C. Her 1995 book *Geisha* won the American Society of Media Photographers Special Achievement Award in 1996. Cobb was the first woman to be named the White House Photographer of the Year. She is currently working on a project exploring international concepts of beauty from Papua, New Guinea, to Moscow. She lives in Washington, D.C.

BENEDICT J. FERNANDEZ was born and raised in New York City. In 1968 he founded the Department of Photography at the New School/Parsons School of Design and was chairman of the department until 1992. He is currently Senior Fellow in Photography at the Corcoran Gallery of Art. He has been a John Simon Guggenheim Fellow, recipient of a National Endowment for the Arts grant, a Fellow of the American Academy of Arts and Sciences, and a Senior Fulbright Scholar. His books include *Protest,* 1996; *I Am a Man,* 1996; *Countdown to Eternity,* 1993; and *In Opposition: The Right to Dissent,* 1968. Fernandez's work is in the collections of the Museum of Modern Art, the Boston Museum of Fine Arts, the National Portrait Gallery, the Corcoran Gallery of Art, and the Bibliothèque Nationale, Paris, among other venues. He lives in North Bergen, New Jersey.

DONNA FERRATO was born in Waltham, Massachusetts. In 1991, after her book *Living with the Enemy* was published, she founded Domestic Abuse Awareness, Inc., to raise funds and educate the public about domestic violence. Her work has been published extensively in *Life, Fortune, The New York Times Magazine, Stern, DAS,* and *Du;* her assignments have ranged from covering Bruce Springsteen to the Persian Gulf War. Her awards include a W. Eugene Smith grant, the Robert F. Kennedy Award for Humanistic Photography, and the Kodak Crystal Eagle for Courage in Journalism. Ferrato lectures on domestic violence at universities, hospitals, and shelters. She lives in New York City.

BETSY FRAMPTON was born in New York City. She received an undergraduate degree from Barnard College, Columbia University, and a graduate degree in Visual Studies from Harvard University in 1970. Frampton has photographed for *Time, Life, Business Week, People, Town and Country,* and *Washingtonian,* among other magazines. Her journalistic assignments have included photographing Peace Corps programs in Nepal, Niger, the Gambia, and Morocco and VISTA programs in West Virginia and California. She was a finalist in the W. Eugene Smith Fellowship Program in 1983 and won numerous awards in the White House News Photographers' Association annual photo contest between 1980 and 1984. Her work is included in the collections of the Smithsonian Institution, the John F. Kennedy Library, and the Library of Congress. She lives in Washington, D.C.

TIPPER GORE, Honorary Chair of *The Way Home: Ending Homelessness in America,* is a major advocate on issues of homelessness, mental health, and the status of women and children. Throughout her life, she has worked on behalf of the homeless and mentally ill, first as a volunteer and founder of advocacy organizations, and more recently on the national level as Mental Health Policy Advisor to the President. A former photojournalist, she has combined her interest in photography and advocacy in this unique project, to help bring this issue to the forefront of our national agenda and educate all Americans on how we can move people out of homelessness into a continuum of care.

ANNIE LEIBOVITZ's portraits have been appearing on magazine covers for more than twenty-five years. Starting with her work for *Rolling Stone* magazine and continuing through a long affiliation with *Vanity Fair* and *Vogue,* she has established herself as an astute observer of American popular culture. In addition to magazine work, Leibovitz has accepted many commissions. She was the official portrait photographer for the World Cup Games in Mexico in 1985, and created prize-winning advertising campaigns for American Express and The Gap. She documented the creation of the White Oak Dance Project for Mikhail Baryshnikov and has worked with many other artistic organizations, including American Ballet Theatre and the Mark Morris Dance Group. During the siege of Sarajevo, Leibovitz visited the city and created a series of portraits that were exhibited in 1993 at the Art Gallery of Bosnia and Herzegovina. In 1995 she was commissioned to create the official portfolio for the Twenty-sixth Olympic Games in Atlanta, Georgia. In 1999 she published *Women,* a book of portraits with an essay by Susan Sontag, accompanying an exhibition at the Corcoran Gallery of Art.

MARY ELLEN MARK received a bachelor of fine arts degree in painting and art history and a master of arts from the Annenberg School of Communication, University of Pennsylvania. Her photo-essays have been published in *Harper's Bazaar, The New York Times Magazine, The New Yorker, Rolling Stone,* and *Vogue,* among other journals. She has received numerous grants and awards, including a John Simon Guggenheim Fellowship, an Erna and Victor Hasselblad Foundation grant, the Creative Arts Awards Citation for Photography from Brandeis University, the George W. Polk Award for Photojournalism, the Infinity Award from the International Center of Photography, and three National Endowment for the Arts grants. Her publications include *Falkland Road,* 1981, *Mother Teresa's Mission of Charity in Calcutta,* 1985, *Streetwise,* 1988 and 1992, *Indian Circus,* 1993, and *Portraits,* 1997. Her most recent book project is *American Odyssey,* a collection of work done in the United States, which accompanies a 2000 exhibition at the Philadelphia Museum of Art. Mary Ellen Mark lives in New York City.

ELI REED was born in Linden, New Jersey, in 1946. He graduated from the Newark School of Fine and Industrial Arts in 1969. He was a Nieman Fellow at Harvard University in 1982–83. Reed worked for *The Middletown* (New York) *Times Herald Record, The Detroit News,* and *The San Francisco Examiner,* before joining the Magnum Photos agency in 1983. His photographs have been featured in *American Photographer, Camera 35, French Photo, Life, National Geographic, Newsweek, Photo District News, Sports Illustrated, Time, Vanity Fair,*

and *Vogue.* He has published two books, *Beirut: City of Regrets,* 1988, and *Black in America,* 1997. Reed's awards include the Overseas Press Club Award, the Leica Medal of Excellence in 1988, the Kodak World Image Award for Fine Photography in 1992, and a W. Eugene Smith Grant in Documentary Photography in 1992. He lives in Brooklyn, New York.

JOSEPH RODRIGUEZ was born in Brooklyn, New York, in 1951. He attended the School of Visual Arts in New York and received an associate degree in applied science from New York City Technical College in 1980 and a photojournalism/documentary diploma from the International Center for Photography in 1985. He is represented by the Black Star Photo Agency, New York, and Mira Bild Arkiv, Sweden, and is also associated with the Pacific News Service. His most recent book, *East Side Stories: Gang Life in East L.A.,* was published in 1998. He is currently working on a project about juvenile crime in San Francisco for the Open Society Institute, using a Crime, Communities, and Culture Media Fellowship. He lives in Brooklyn, New York.

STEPHEN SHAMES is a freelance photojournalist specializing in social issues and highlighting solutions. His first book, *Outside the Dream: Child Poverty in America,* was published in 1991. A second book, *Pursuing the Dream: What Helps Children and Their Families Succeed,* was published in 1997. Shames's recent projects include a book on multiracial people and a video on violence prevention, featuring Friends of the Children. Among his awards are the Kodak Crystal Eagle, the Leica Medal of Excellence in Photojournalism, and the Robert F. Kennedy Journalism Award. He founded the Outside the Dream Foundation, which develops public-education programs. Shames lives in Brooklyn, New York.

CALLIE SHELL was born in Gainesville, Georgia, in 1961 and graduated from the College of Charleston in 1983, with a bachelor of arts degree in political science. She has worked as a staff photographer for *USA*

Today, The Tennessean, and *The Pittsburgh Press,* and is now a White House photographer. Her work has been published in *Newsweek, Time, Paris Match,* and *Life* magazines. She has received several awards in education from the National Press Photographers' Association. Shell lives in Washington, D.C.

DIANA WALKER is a contract photographer for *Time* magazine, covering the White House. A graduate of Briarcliff College, where she majored in drama, she has photographed the Reagan, Bush, and Clinton administrations. For the last six years she has specialized in black-and-white behind-the-scenes picture essays of President Clinton, Vice President Gore, Hillary Rodham Clinton, Tipper Gore, and various members of the Clinton-Gore administration, which have appeared in *Time.* She has won numerous awards from the White House News Photographers' Association, including first prize in the Presidential category for the past four years, the National Press Photographers' Association, the Page One Awards, and World Press Photo. Walker's work is in the collections of the National Portrait Gallery, the Art Institute of Chicago, and the Minneapolis Museum of Art. She lives in Washington, D.C.

CLARENCE WILLIAMS was born in Philadelphia in 1967. He attended Temple University, majoring in mass communications. As a photojournalist, he has earned numerous awards, including the Pulitzer Prize for feature photography in 1998 for work that accompanied the *Los Angeles Times* series Orphans of Addiction. He has also received the National Press Photographers Association Award and the Robert F. Kennedy Award for domestic photojournalism, and has been named Times-Mirror Journalist of the Year and Journalist of the Year of the National Association of Black Journalists. Williams has been a staff photographer for *The Los Angeles Times* since 1996. He lives in Los Angeles.

ACKNOWLEDGMENTS

The exhibition and publication *The Way Home: Ending Homelessness in America* explore ways to eliminate one of our most urgent social problems. Work on this educational project has been characterized by a single-minded devotion to meeting this goal on the part of many selfless people. It would not have been possible to undertake such a complex endeavor without their thoughtful encouragement and assistance. We are particularly grateful to Dr. David C. Levy, President and Director of the Corcoran Gallery of Art; Paul Gottlieb, Editor in Chief of Harry N. Abrams, Inc.; and Susan Baker and Eli Segal, Co-Chairs of the Board of the National Alliance to End Homelessness, for their extraordinary support of this project; and also to its distinguished National Advisory Committee, co-chaired by Senator Pete Domenici and Nancy Domenici.

We are most indebted to the talented photographers who have very generously participated in this important project: Jodi Cobb, Benedict J. Fernandez, Donna Ferrato, Betsy Frampton, Tipper Gore, Annie Leibovitz, Mary Ellen Mark, Eli Reed, Joseph Rodriguez, Stephen Shames, Callie Shell, Diana Walker, and Clarence Williams. We are also deeply grateful to Neal Avery, Jr., Gregory Hill, Larry Kyle, James Mann, Larry Mitchell, Elizabeth Anne Newton, Randolph Shaird, Lee Stringer, and an anonymous author for the powerful poems that accompany the images.

For their work on the production of the exhibition and book we would like to specially thank the following people from the Corcoran Gallery of Art: Dena Andre, David Applegate, Ken Ashton, Susan Badder, Heather Berg, Deborah Berman, the Bonner Group, Steve Brown, Jack Cowart, Yvonne Dailey, Sara Durr, Ann Louise Elliott, Victoria Fisher, Cathy Frankel, Katherine Keane, Elizabeth Parr, Paul Roth, Jan Rothschild, and Margaret Wieners.

We must give particular recognition to the publisher, Harry N. Abrams, Inc., and are indebted to Eve Sinaiko, who edited this book, Ana Rogers, who designed it, and to Dirk Luykx, Robyn Liverant, and Elizabeth Robbins.

We would like to express our deep appreciation to the staff of the National Alliance to End Homelessness and to the agencies and other service providers pictured and named in this volume, who graciously opened their doors to the photographers during the project and whose assistance in organizing site visits was invaluable. We wish especially to thank Paula Van Ness, Sue Suh, Kirk Gibson, Suzanne Mintz, Steve Berg, Stephen Coyle, Susan Davis, Barbara Easterling, Anthony Harrington, and David Warnock; Xavier de Souza Briggs, Jim Hoben, Fred Karnas, Jacquie Lawing, Mary Ellen O'Connell, and Marsha Martin, the National Mental Health Association. The dedicated representatives of homeless service organizations around the country have our gratitude, and we must mention in particular Ruth Dickey, Teresa Connell, Jane Graf, Mandy Nelson, Hilda Fernandez, Olga Golik, Lynn Summers, Dr. Jim O'Connell, Katy Gingles, Philip Mangano, Shepley Metcalf, Aimee Molloy, Colonel Charles Williams, Cynthia Wilson, Sally Shipman, Michael Dahl, Sue Watlov Phillips, Karen Dawson, Tanya Tull, Bud Hayes, Della Mitchell, Jean Butzen, Rosanne Haggerty, Leo Paradis, Kathy Oliver, and Ray Tullius.

Philip Brookman
Nan Roman
Jane Slate Siena

PHOTOGRAPHERS' ACKNOWLEDGMENTS

I would like to thank Livia Garcia, City of Miami, Office of Homeless Programs; Al Brown, Homeless Assistance Center, Miami; Olga Golik and Charles Flowers, Douglas Gardens Community Mental Health Center of Miami Beach; and outreach workers Albert Eusebio, Michael Hankerson, Lloyd Williams, Guillermo Rodriguez, and William Harris, with City of Miami Outreach.

Jodi Cobb

I would like to acknowledge and thank all the organizations that helped me in Houston, especially Project SEARCH, and the people who permitted me to photograph them, as well as my friends.

Benedict J. Fernandez

Thank you to Della Mitchell, Dolly Brewer, and the staff of the Olive Branch Mission, including Executive Director David Bates. I also thank the remarkable women I met, Margie Garrett and Denise Miller.

Donna Ferrato

I thank Katy Gingles, Dr. Jim O'Connell, Sharon Morrison, and Cheryl Kane from the Boston Health Care for the Homeless program; Shepley Metcalf from Pine Street Inn; Macy DeLong, Executive Director, Solutions at Work; Michael J. Sullivan from Bread and Jams; Reverend Debbie Little from Common Cathedral; and Philip Mangano from the Massachusetts Housing and Shelter Alliance.

Betsy Frampton

I would like to acknowledge the network of activists, caregivers, and ordinary citizens who have found lasting solutions to homelessness through quiet efforts on behalf of struggling individuals and families. And most of all, I would like to acknowledge the men, women, and children who, through whatever circumstance, find themselves living on the streets. They are truly courageous and skillful survivors who are worthy of our caring, understanding, and compassion.

Tipper Gore

I wish to thank Rosanne Haggerty, Director, Common Ground; and Cynthia Dial and Richard Schwartz from Project FIND and the Woodstock Hotel.

Annie Leibovitz

I thank Maria Cuomo, Joanne Leonhardt Cassullo, HELP USA, and Peter Howe.

Mary Ellen Mark

I would like to thank Kristin Treiber, Rick Rocamora, Jen Cheeks, and Suzanne Locke for their contributions to my project.

Eli Reed

I would like to thank Sue Watlov Phillips, from Elim Transitional Housing, and Greg Horan, who worked so hard to help me meet people in Minneapolis and St. Paul. Most importantly, I'd like to thank all the families and individuals who let me into their lives.

Joseph Rodriguez

Thank you to Dorral Coral, Larry Martínez, Isabel Delgado, Jennifer Case, Maria Poniagua, Damariz Macias, Silvia Sierra, Edwina Moses, Janet Spector Bishop, Stacy French Reynolds, Steve Rudolph, Joyce Grengert, Dean Rennie, Ray Tullius, the staff and clients at Lakefront SRO, Enunciation House, the Child Crisis Center, El Paso Center for Children, the YMCA's Transitional Living Center, L. A. Nixon Elementary School, SCRAP METTLE/Soul, Universal Geriatric Services, UPS, Amy Snyder, Reuben Casteñada, Maria Jesse, Debra Brown, and Lien Lee.

Stephen Shames

I would like to thank Karen Dawson and Seattle YWCA; the women and staff of Angeline's; the staff, students, and volunteers of First Place; the women and staff of Hammond House Women's Shelter; Broadview Emergency Shelter; Delores Hillis and Seattle Emergency Housing; Diane Powers with the YMCA; Georgette, Tairrie, Torrance, and Marshelle; Pamela, Joseph, and Xzavier Miller; Chris Rennebohm and Barbara Benton; Valerie and Lisa.

Callie Shell

Thanks to Arthelia Finnie of the Arlington-Alexandria Coalition for the Homeless, Inc.; Aimee Molloy of the Center for Poverty Solutions, Baltimore; and Colonel Charles Williams and Colonel Walter Mitchell of the Maryland Center for Veterans Education and Training, Inc.

Diana Walker

Thanks to Gilbert, Leonard, and Kelly for opening their lives to me, to my parents for their support, and to Carolyn, Frank, Genaro, and Rob for their friendship, guidance, and love.

Clarence Williams